DALMATIAN COOKING
Cuisine of the Slavic Mediterranean

John J. Goddard

ISBN: 1468166182
ISBN-13: 978-1468166187

DEDICATION

For my grandmother, Mary Beth Welby.

CONTENTS

Acknowledgments

I.   Foreword   8

II.   Gastronomy and History   11

III. The Dalmatian Kitchen   15

IV.   Soups   22

V.   Vegetables and Accompaniments   51

VI.   Pasta, Rice and Dumplings   72

VII. Salads   99

VIII. Fish and Seafood   107

IX.   Meat, Fowl and Game   165

X.   Sauces and Condiments   243

XI.   Sweets   253

ACKNOWLEDGMENTS

My gratitude goes out to the many people of Croatia who shared their cookbooks, family recipes, time, patience and knowledge with me. Without these, this book would not have been possible. I must also acknowledge the work of Dika Marjanović Radica. Her classic tome of Dalmatian recipes *Dalmatinska Kuhinja* has become an invaluable source of knowledge and inspiration.

I. FOREWORD

My goal in presenting this book is the transmission of a cultural heritage. It is hoped that when you read this book, you will not only gain knowledge of Dalmatian recipes and cooking techniques, but also some insight into the history and unique perspectives behind them. Rather than simply provide you with detailed instructions for cooking dishes, this book aims to give an understanding of the cuisine as a whole, and hopefully an appreciation of its origins and philosophy. Dalmatian cuisine embodies the ideal of elegance in simplicity. It is an elemental cuisine driven more by ingredients than elaborate technique, focused on allowing the natural quality and nutritional value of ingredients to shine. This simplicity and economy of approach is, I believe, the cornerstone of its charm, and the reason I first felt strongly about writing this book.

Modern cookbooks tend to provide excruciatingly detailed methods for reproducing dishes exactly, or, more specific to this industrial age, for the *manufacture* of dishes. Little regard is given for the origin of the dish, the nuances of its preparation, or the character of its prescriber. My goal is not to modernize the recipes contained here, but to present them as I have received them. I have translated them from the Croatian language and its Dalmatian dialect as faithfully as I am able, giving consideration for cultural idiosyncrasy where necessary for the sake of understanding.

There is a quaint charm to be found in old recipes, and I have not sought to paint over the unique character of those contained in this book. They were handed down through generations, in many cases adapted to relatively modern measuring standards after hundreds of years of use. I have left the measurements in their original metric, which is not only more widely used around the world, but also a more precise system for culinary purposes. One can easily find an inexpensive kitchen scale to measure in metric, and I hope you will do just that. In the third chapter I give simple equivalents for the metric units of measurement for those who are not familiar.

You will notice, however, that exact measurements for many ingredients are simply not given. Those who find this an impassable obstacle should perhaps not be trusted to prepare food, since they do not trust themselves. Dalmatians cook with their eyes, hands and tastebuds, just as most of the world's chefs and grandmothers. As a teacher, I value this nonspecific approach to the information; it forces the student to become acquainted with the properties and behaviors of ingredients, the nature of a dish and the variables involved in the execution.

The procedures for preparing the dishes are given as short descriptions rather than minutely detailed instructions. On one hand, this is the result of my efforts to present the recipes as faithfully as possible, for this is how they were originally written. It is a better format for absorbing and retaining the information as a whole, and one embraced by the great chef Escoffier for the cooking instruction in his masterpiece *Le Guide Culinaire*. Gather your ingredients, then read through the instructions to the end. Visualize each step of preparation and the finished dish before you touch a knife or pot. When you have a mental image of the desired end result, you will have a sense of what must be done to achieve it. If you wish to become a better cook, then you should strive for intuition and common sense in the kitchen, whether you are cooking Dalmatian cuisine or any other. In that respect, this book presents you with a collection of lessons to master in your kitchen. I contend that this is how all cooking should be approached. The end result may not always be exactly what you planned, but if it is tasty and satisfying, then you have not failed. Take notes and make the necessary adjustments the next time you prepare the dish. A book's aim should be to guide you through a learning experience, not dictate exactly how it should and will go. If, however, you have questions or need advice in preparing a specific dish, I encourage you to contact me directly through the website dalmatiancooking.com, or post your question on the Facebook page, Dalmatian Cooking.

Dalmatian cuisine is generally very simple to prepare. It is not terribly complex or exotic, and so it is not only widely appealing, but also an excellent culinary idiom within which to practice and develop kitchen skills. I encourage you to do just that, and to experiment, innovate and build on the recipes presented here if you so desire.

Cook wildly and happily.

II. GASTRONOMY AND HISTORY

Dalmatia is a region of current southwestern Croatia on the coast of the Adriatic Sea. Its cuisine is defined partly by ingredients that grow well in the Mediterranean climate, such as olives, almonds, figs, grapes, wild herbs, vegetables and citrus fruit. A wide variety of fish species are also plentiful in the pristine waters of the lakes, rivers and sea, and seafood figures very prominently into the diet. Due to the ingredients and methods of preparation, Dalmatian cuisine is considered especially healthy, meeting all nutritional and medical recommendations for a well balanced diet.

A vibrant winemaking tradition has existed since ancient times in the region, and some Dalmatian wines are considered among the world's finest. Celebrated wines include Dingač and Posip from the Pelješac Peninsula, Babić from Primošten, Vugava from the isle of Hvar, Grk from the isle of Korčula, Marastina from the isle of Lastovo, and Malvazija from Dubrovnik. The most widely cultivated grape variety is the ancient Plavac Mali, which is related to the Zinfandel grape.

Strong fruit brandies are also distilled, primarily from the abundant grapes of the region, and they are flavored with a variety of plants and herbs. The king of all brandies in Dalmatia is travarica, a sophisticated spirit that serves as a superb digestive tonic. It is quite simply an infusion of pure grape brandy and a variety of herbs, and there are as many recipes for travarica as there are people producing it. Some varieties contain as few as ten herbs, while others can contain twenty or more. Plant materials typically added to the brandy include rosemary, chamomile, lavender, rose hips, matgrass, juniper, thyme, currants, mint and sage.

Wines and brandies are not only sipped, but also used extensively in cooking as you will see.

There are also millennia of tumultuous history influencing the flavors of Dalmatian cuisine, written in part by the Illyrians, Greeks, Romans, Slavs, Italians, Austrians, Hungarians and Ottoman Turks who have occupied its islands, hills and shores. That there were ancient Greek and Phœnician colonies along the coast and on the islands is certain; the earliest of the former was that founded by the Syracusans on the isle of Vis around 390 B.C. Celts were also in the region around this time.

Dalmatia's name comes from that of an Illyrian tribe, the Dalmatae, who later lived in the area. Dalmatian history began officially when this tribe declared itself independent from the Illyrian king Gentius in 180 B.C., and claimed the land as their own. The Roman Empire began its occupation of the region in 168 B.C., establishing the province of Illyricum. The capital was Salona, near what is now the city of Split. Illyricum stretched from the Drin River in Albania to modern Istria in the northwest, and to the Sava River in the north.

By the time the Western Roman Empire collapsed in 476 A.D., Dalmatia was fully Latinized. It was thereafter ruled by Goths until 535, when it was added to the Byzantine Empire by Justinian I. It was around this time that tribes of Slavic Croats migrated and settled Dalmatia and its surrounding lands, forming the Principality of Littoral Croatia. This was ruled by Slavic princes and kings until 1097, and received protection from the Byzantine Empire, then Venice and Hungary. During the whole of the 12th century Venice and Hungary contested the possession of Dalmatia, victory inclining to Venice, who, by policing the Adriatic, made her protection valuable to the coastal cities. Venetian influence and control increased continually, and Hungary was forced to abandon any claim on the territory when it had to protect its own lands from the Ottoman Turks, who swept through Europe in the 15th century. By the next century, the Turks were able to conquer most of the Dalmatian hinterland, while the coastal towns and islands remained in the hands of Venice. Thus the frontiers of the two empires met, and war was nearly continuous until the Turks were driven out in the late 17th century.

Venice ruled Dalmatia until 1797, when the Venetian Empire collapsed under Napolean Bonaparte. In the terms of the Treaty of Campo Formio between France and Austria that same year, Napolean gave control of Dalmatia to Austria. In 1805 Dalmatia was given back to France, and became part of Napolean's Kingdom of Italy. The region shifted between French and Austrian hands several times until 1815, when the Habsurgs finally established firm control. Though there were continuous political struggles with the local Croat majority who desired autonomy, Austria retained rule over Dalmatia until World War I, when the Austro-Hungarian Empire was defeated and dissolved.

The Treaty of London in 1915 then gave northern Dalmatia and some of the islands to Italy, while the south went to the Kingdom of Serbia. In 1918 the Kingdom of Serbs, Croats and Slovenes (also known as the Kingdom of Yugoslavia) was established, and southern Dalmatia remained in Slavic hands until 1941, when Axis forces invaded and conquered Yugoslavia during World War II. Most of Dalmatia was handed back to Italy, and the rest was ruled by the Independent State of Croatia, a fascist puppet state of Nazi Germany. In 1944, the local Partisan resistance movement of Josip Broz Tito retook Dalmatia from the fascists, and most of the Italian population fled the region. Croatia then became a republic within Tito's newly established Socialist Federal Republic of Yugoslavia after World War II, and the region historically considered Dalmatia was almost entirely within its new borders.

Upon Tito's death in 1980, ethnic nationalism in the Yugoslavian states swelled. Yugoslavia began to dissolve, and Croatia declared its independence in 1991. It remains an independent republic to this day.

Throughout history the influences of every culture and conqueror mentioned in this chapter (and especially Italy) left their mark on Dalmatia's Mediterranean style of cooking, and this much loved cuisine is but one important aspect of Croatian cultural identity.

III. THE DALMATIAN KITCHEN

In many cases, the traditional Dalmatian kitchen itself might comprise a dedicated room within the home for ingredient preparation, plus a free-standing enclosed structure outside of the home within which cooking on wood fire and the smoking of meat and fish can be done. This separate structure would contain a low stone or masonry platform about the size of a small bed. Upon this platform, wood fires are built and used in conjunction with a variety of utensils for grilling, roasting, stewing and baking. Cured meats and sausages might be hung within to age and passively take up the flavors and preservative properties of ambient smoke. A variety of forged iron utensils would also hang from the walls and ceiling. Smaller free-standing structures for cooking on wood fire are simple stone or masonry platforms with a tiled roof and a chimney.

You will be able to execute the recipes with common kitchen equipment, but cooking with wood fire and traditional utensils is a very large part of real Dalmatian cooking. If you would like assistance with locating and purchasing these items, simply express your wishes through the website dalmatiancooking.com.

TOOLS AND UTENSILS

Pot stand – This is a simple raised circular platform on three short legs upon which to place a variety of pots and pans over wood fire. It is generally made of iron or steel.

Braising pan – The braising pan is perhaps the most commonly used cooking vessel in the Dalmatian kitchen, as the cuisine features many meat and fish stews that are slow cooked in large quantities for long periods of time. It is about three times as wide as it is deep, and made of steel or enameled metal.

Stock pot – The stock pot is also used for soups and stews. In some homes you might find smaller stock pots with a wire handle arching over the top. These can be suspended over fire with a chain hanging from a tripod.

Grill – Grilling over wood fire is a very important aspect of Dalmatian cuisine. The variety most commonly used is Tuscan-style, made of iron. The square grillwork is raised on four short legs so that it can stand on its own over glowing embers.

Peka - The peka is a large metal or clay baking dome that has been in use since the time of the ancient Illyrians. Anything of the recipes you find in this book that call for roast or bake – even some breads and cakes – can be cooked under the peka. The dome is placed on the pot stand over wood fire to begin heating it. A metal or clay plate is filled with ingredients such as meat, fish and vegetables. When the wood has burned to large embers and the dome is hot, the plate of food is placed on the cooking platform and covered with the dome. The embers are then raked on top of the dome to provide indirect heat to the ingredients within. Since the cooking chamber created is essentially airtight, roasted foods remain juicy and succulent. Roasting under the peka yields excellent results. The vegetables most commonly cooked together with the main protein are potatoes, onions and carrots. The peka is a central aspect of Dalmatians' cultural identity, and one of which they are very proud.

Food mill – Many of the recipes included in this book were recorded before the invention of modern electrical kitchen equipment, such as blenders and food processors. Dalmatian cuisine does feature sauces that are coarsely pureed by means of a food mill, but you may of course use modern devices to achieve the desired result. The food mill is a hand-operated device placed over a bowl. Cooked ingredients are placed into the mill, and they are forced through a meshwork by means of a hand crank.

Meat grinder – You will notice a marked difference in the quality of the ground meat dishes you prepare when you select and grind the cuts yourself. Recipes for sausages, stuffed cabbage and more call for ground meat. The old fashioned hand-cranked type of meat grinder is an inexpensive addition to your kitchen, and the extra effort you will put into your cooking by using this device will shine through. Of course, you may simply visit your butcher and request certain cuts to be ground to the desired consistency.

INGREDIENTS

VEGETABLES

Vegetables for soup – When a recipe calls for "vegetables for soup," this refers to aromatics such as parsley and celery roots and leaves, carrots and kale. These are commonly sold bundled together throughout Croatia.

Onions and garlic – These feature very prominently in the cuisine, as you will see. Many recipes begin with frying onions in fat, and garlic is often minced finely with smoked bacon and parsley leaves to make a flavor-enhancing paste.

Pickled cabbage – Essentially, this is sauerkraut, but cabbage heads are usually fermented and sold whole in the region. When a recipe calls for shredded sauerkraut, one would simply slice the whole leaves very finely into strips. The whole leaves are generally rolled around minced meat, rice and other ingredients, then baked slowly with smoked pork and perhaps tomato sauce. A good Eastern European grocer will stock whole heads of pickled cabbage.

Capers – The Mediterranean climate of Dalmatia is the perfect environment for capers to grow wild. They are often used to enhance the flavor of dishes as an ingredient or garnish.

Olives – The Dalmatian coast has been an area of olive cultivation for over a thousand years. Cured olives are eaten alone with cold meats and cheeses, or chopped and added to stews and sauces.

Pickled shallots and onions – Shallots and onions are pickled in simply seasoned red wine vinegar. They are served as a relish with cold meats.

Herbs – The most common herbs used in Dalmatian cuisine are parsley, rosemary and sage, as they grow quite abundantly in the local climate.

Tomato Paste – This is widely used to build and enrich sauces.

PROTEINS

Smoked dry bacon – Known as *panceta* in Dalmatia, dry cured, smoked pork belly is used extensively in the kitchen. It is different than common bacon in that it is not cooked, and it contains nearly no moisture. In addition to cooking uses, it can be sliced thinly and eaten as it is with other smoked meats and sausages as an appetizer or snack.

Smoked and dried meats – Pork, beef and mutton are all salt cured, smoked and dried for long storage. Whole cuts might be rehydrated and stewed later, or cut into pieces and cooked with beans or in soups. The best loved of all cured meats in Dalmatia is *pršut*, which is the regional version of prosciutto ham. Unlike common Italian prosciuttos, *pršut* is often smoked.

Salt cured fish – Sardines and anchovies are extremely plentiful in the waters of the Adriatic Sea, and they are cured in large quantities for long storage. In addition to being eaten with bread, olives and cheese as an appetizer or snack, the cured filets are added to many dishes to enhance flavor and richness.

LIPIDS AND LIQUIDS

Olive oil – Dalmatian olive oil is among the finest in the world, but very rarely exported from Croatia. Olive oil is used in cooking and salads, and drizzled over prepared dishes as a condiment.

Rendered fat – You will notice that many recipes in this book call for cooking with fat. While this would generally mean rendered lard or bacon drippings in Dalmatia, you may substitute shortening or oil if desired.

Hard Cheese – Parmesan and Grana Padano are often grated over dishes or used to make sauces.

Broth – Many recipes call for the addition of broth or soup stock. Dalmatian cooking calls for much boiling or poaching of foods, so there is nearly always some manner of broth on hand. It is good practice in any kitchen or cuisine to maintain a little store of broth for cooking, especially vegetable broth since it can be used with any meat, fish or poultry dish. Simply simmer soup vegetables in water with a bay leaf and a few peppercorns until you achieve a good, flavorful strength, then strain out the solids and refrigerate until needed.

Wine – Many families still make their own wine in Dalmatia, or simply buy or barter for it with a neighbor who does. Wine is plentiful enough to cook with often, and liberally. Cooking fish stews in pure, unadulterated wine is not at all unheard of.

Vinegar – Where there is wine, there will be vinegar. Red wine vinegar is the preferred variety for use in recipes, but white vinegar can be used as well.

MEASUREMENTS

Kilogram (kg) – A kilogram is 1000 grams. One kilogram is equal to 2.2 pounds.

Dekagram (dag) – A dekagram is 10 grams. Three dekagrams are approximately equal to 1 ounce. Since most metric kitchen scales weigh in grams, simply add a zero to the number of dekagrams given for an ingredient to calculate the number of grams needed.

Liter (L) – One liter is approximately equal to 34 fluid ounces.

Deciliter (dL) – A deciliter is one tenth of a liter. It is therefore approximately equal to 3.4 fluid ounces.

Teaspoon and Tablespoon (tsp. and tbsp.) – In the case of the recipes in this book, *teaspoon* and *tablespoon* do not necessarily refer to the exact units of measurement. In the original Croatian versions, these usually meant 'small spoon' and 'large spoon' respectively. I have used the common abbreviations.

Cup – As used in this book, the term *cup* also does not refer to the exact unit of measurement, but rather to a coffee or tea cup.

IV. SOUPS

Soup is nearly always served at or near the beginning of a full meal in Dalmatia, or as a light meal unto itself. Its purpose is stimulating the appetite and beginning the task of filling the belly. While in the West soups are generally thicker, Dalmatian soups are often simple, flavorful broths, and they do not always include the meat or vegetables that were cooked in them. Soup can be as much a byproduct of cooking meat, poultry, fish or vegetables by boiling as it is an intentional result. Some is kept on hand not only to be used as a course for meals, but also as an ingredient in other dishes and sauces that call for stock. Few can argue the wisdom of keeping a pot of vegetable stock on hand at all times for cooking.

Beef broth is a favorite, but chicken, veal, fish and shellfish, vegetables and legumes all make appearances. The soup can be served as an unembellished liquid, or with a variety of fortifications and additives, such as pasta, rice or dumplings.

Eggs or egg yolks are also added to give a soup richness and body. If the yolk alone is used, simply place it in the bottom of the bowl, then pour hot broth over it while stirring to incorporate. When adding whole eggs, it is best to whisk them into a cold liquid first, then incorporate this liquid into hot soup. In this way you are assured a smooth, even consistency.

Meat soups are usually begun by adding meat to cold, unsalted water, then heated. When the water comes to a boil, vegetables, roots, herbs, spices and salt are added. The heat is reduced and the soup is allowed to simmer for several hours. Use 15-20 dekagrams of meat and 1.5 liters of water per person. When the soup is cooked to a good strength, remove all solids and set aside. Skim any fat that has risen to the surface, add a bit of cold water to the broth, then strain through fine mesh. Heat the broth again and add pasta, dumplings or rice as desired. Meat and vegetables can then be portioned into soup bowls and the hot soup ladled thereupon.

Beef soup should cook for 3-4 hours at a slow, even rate. It will become cloudy if it is cooked too quickly. The foam of protein is seldom skimmed off due to its nutritional value, but rather stirred into the broth. Chicken soup is cooked in a similar fashion, with half a chicken providing enough soup and meat for four people.

Soup can be made simply from beef or veal bones, especially those from the spine, which boast high nutritional value. Roast the bones in the oven until a deep brown caramelization is achieved, then sauté roughly chopped onions, garlic, carrots and celery with a few peppercorns in fat or oil. Add the bones and vegetables to a pot of warm water, bring to a boil, then add salt and simmer for 2-3 hours. Strain the broth through a fine mesh and proceed with additional ingredients as desired.

Meatless soups often begin with a thin roux consisting of one tablespoon of warm rendered fat and a half tablespoon of flour per person. It can also be made with butter, olive or vegetable oil in the same proportions. Heat the fat, butter or oil in a pan, frying a bit of chopped onion therein if desired. Then stir in the flour over low heat until well incorporated into the oil. Cold water can be stirred into the roux before adding it to hot soup to prevent the formation of lumps. Meatless soups often receive the benefit of some cubed bread which has been fried or toasted like croutons.

Soups with rice, grains, noodles or dumplings are also well loved in Dalmatia. Rice should be added in the final 15-20 minutes of cooking in a measure of 5 dekagrams per person, or about half a teacup. Barley can be added in similar proportion, but will require at least an hour to cook. Semolina requires a scant 10 minutes of cooking. Grains impart greater flavor when they have been lightly toasted in a skillet with a bit of fat before adding to the soup.

Pastas are traditionally prepared from scratch as needed, rather than purchased dry from the market. You will certainly appreciate the difference a little extra time and effort can make. To make a good pasta dough, add 2 eggs and a few tablespoons of water to 20 dekagrams of flour. Mix well, then knead for at least ten minutes to get a firm, elastic dough. Roll, cut and shape as desired. This quantity of dough will make enough pasta for four people.

Soup from Bones

50 dag beef or veal bones
1 tbsp. fat
celery root and leaves
parsley root
2-3 carrots
½ onion
5 peppercorns
2 L warm water
salt

Melt the fat in the bottom of a stock pot. Add the bones, some chopped celery leaves, sliced celery and parsley root, onion, carrots and a few peppercorns. Brown all of this well over a high flame, then add 2 liters of water and bring to a boil. Add salt, reduce heat to a simmer and cook for two hours. Pasta or dumplings can be added as desired.

Ujušak

diced meat or fowl
fat
1 onion
1 carrot
celery root
salt and pepper
broth or water
a bit of tomato paste
parsley

Heat some fat in a saucepan, add chopped onion and fry. Add a little water and fry a little more until you have a nice golden color. Add the meat or poultry, stir well, cover and allow to simmer. When this becomes juicy, add chopped carrot and celery root, broth or water and pepper. Cover and allow to simmer until all is tender. Stir in a spoonful or two of flour and mix it well into the meat and vegetables. Add plenty of broth or water and some tomato paste, season to taste with salt and allow to simmer for half an hour to an hour. Before serving, add chopped parsley. Serve with a light side dish or gnocchi.

Chicken Soup

1 hen or cock
celery root
carrots
1 small onion
salt and pepper
chicken giblets (heart, liver, gizzards)
1 tbsp. fat
½ onion, chopped
tomato paste or diced tomatoes
rice (half a teacup per person)
grated hard cheese
parsley

Remove the feathers, head, feet and innards of the bird. Cut the wings and legs from the body, then wash these well with cold water. Put the body, legs and wings in cold water and bring to a boil, then add whole carrots, a small onion cut in quarters, a bit of sliced celery root, salt and a small handful of peppercorns. Reduce heat and simmer for two hours or so. While the bird is cooking, periodically add more cold water to the pot. When the meat is well cooked, pour two small glasses of brandy. Add one to the pot and drink the other.

Wash and chop the giblets finely. Brown the chopped half onion in fat in a separate skillet, then add the giblets and sauté, adding a little chicken broth and tomato paste to the pan and simmer. When the giblets are well cooked, add them to the pot with rice and simmer until the rice is cooked, about fifteen minutes. Sprinkle each serving with grated hard cheese and chopped parsley.

Chicken or Veal Stew

chicken or veal
vegetables for soup (celery, carrots, onions, parsley root)
fat
flour
young peas
a few sliced carrots
a cauliflower cut in small pieces
chicken livers

Wash the chicken well and cut into pieces. Fry the chicken pieces and chopped livers in a bit of fat, then put them into a pot with soup vegetables, cover with water and bring to the boil. Reduce heat, season with salt and simmer for two hours. Remove the chicken pieces from the pot and take all of the meat from the bones, then return the meat to the broth. Reheat the rendered fat from frying and add flour to make a light roux. Stir this into the pot with the peas and sliced vegetables and stir well. Simmer until vegetables are tender and the broth has thickened a little. Veal stew may be prepared in the same way.

Brain Soup

1 lamb or ½ calf's brain
5 dag fat
1 small onion, finely chopped
4 dag flour
salt and pepper
1 thick slice of bread, soaked in milk
chopped parsley

Gently parboil the brain in simmering salted water for about five minutes, or just until the proteins have set and the brain holds its shape. Rinse in cold water, remove the veins and dice into small cubes. Fry the chopped red onion in one half ounce of the fat in a skillet until soft and translucent, then add the diced brain and a little salt and pepper (you may also add some finely chopped garlic and dried red pepper flakes at this time of you wish). Fry the brain with the chopped onion until it begins to brown, stirring constantly. Remove from flame and set aside.

Heat the remaining fat over low flame in a saucepan and stir in the flour to make a roux. Continue to heat and stir the roux over medium low flame until it begins to brown. Add the fried brain and onion to the roux, then add 2 liters of water and bring to a low boil. Stir in the soaked bread, add salt and pepper to taste. Reduce heat and simmer for approximately 30 minutes. Add a bit of chopped parsley and serve.

Zelena Manistra *(Green Minnestrone)*

50 dag Brussels sprouts
30-40 dag dried pork and mutton
25 dag potatoes, peeled and large diced
salt and pepper
a few small zucchini
2 tbsp. olive oil
5 dag dry bacon
4 cloves of garlic
parsley
dry sausage

Cut the sprouts in half lengthwise, wash well, parboil in salted water and drain. Wash the dried meat in warm water, then simmer alone in water. When the meat is tender, remove it from the broth and set aside. Add the potatoes to the broth and simmer. When they are half cooked, add the sprouts and cook over low heat for nearly an hour. Taste and adjust the seasoning with salt and pepper. Cut the zucchini into large pieces and add to the broth. Make a chopped paste of the bacon, garlic and parsley. Fry this with sliced sausage and add to the pot, along with the cooked pork and mutton. Stir the olive oil into the broth and serve.

Pašta Fažol

1 kg dried pork or a ham bone
50 dag dry beans
3 tbsp. fat
1 onion, chopped
pepper
6 dag dry bacon
1 clove garlic
parsley
25 dag pasta

Soak the beans and dried pork overnight. Discard the water. Boil the dried pork or ham bone in 3 liters of water. When the pork is half cooked (or the broth has taken on the flavor of the ham bone), add the beans and cook until tender. Make a paste of the bacon, garlic and parsley and fry it in the fat with the onion and pepper. Add this to the broth with the pasta. Simmer until the pasta is cooked.

Autumn Soup

50 dag dried mutton or 75 dag dried beef
1 head of cabbage
a few potatoes
12 dag dry bacon
4 cloves of garlic
parsley

Cook the dried mutton or beef in plenty of water. When the meat is tender (approximately 2 hours) add the cabbage, which you have cut into 8 pieces, and thickly sliced potatoes. Make a chopped paste of the bacon, garlic and parsley, add to the broth and simmer for 10-15 minutes. Cook until the vegetables are tender and serve.

Bean and Sauerkraut Soup

1 kg sauerkraut
3 tbsp. fat
1 red onion
40 dag smoked pork
25 dag beans
grated horseradish

Rinse the sauerkraut well, and fry in the fat with chopped onion in a pot. Cut the dried pork into spoon-sized pieces, wash well in warm water and add to the sauerkraut. Cover with water and simmer on low heat. Cook the beans separately in unsalted water until tender, then add to the sauerkraut, stir well and simmer until the broth has reduced. Serve with grated horseradish or pickled shallots.

Barley Soup with Smoked Meat

1 kg of smoked ham or sausage
25 dag barley
1 tbsp. fat
1 onion
dry bacon
2 cloves of garlic
parsley
2 boiled potatoes

Wash the smoked ham or sausage in warm water, then simmer in 2-3 liters of water until tender. Wash the barley well then fry with chopped onion in a new pot. Strain the broth from the cooked meat into the barley. Make a paste of finely chopped bacon, parsley and garlic and stir this into the soup. Simmer gently for 2 hours, adding a little water if necessary. Finally, crush the boiled potatoes through a sieve and mix them into the soup. Simmer for a bit, then serve.

Barley Soup with Beans

50 dag fresh beef
50 dag dried pork
35 dag barley
35 dag beans
salt
2-3 potatoes
10 dag dry bacon
2-3 cloves of garlic
parsley

Put the beef, pork, barley and beans into a pot, pour cold water to the top, cover and simmer for 2 hours. Add large diced potatoes and season with salt if needed. Make a paste of finely chopped bacon, garlic and parsley, add to the broth and cook for another hour.

Barley Soup with Kaštradina

1 kg dry smoked mutton
vegetables for soup
1 tbsp. fat
50 dag barley
2 potatoes

Wash the mutton well in warm water and boil well with soup vegetables. Toast the barley in a skillet with the fat and add to the soup with sliced potatoes. Cook for 2 hours. Serve with braised sauerkraut or a pickled salad.

MEATLESS SOUPS

Spring Soup

50 dag green peas
25 dag potatoes
5 tbsp. olive oil
2 tbsp. flour
½ onion
2 cloves garlic
parsley and celery leaves
3 carrots
1 tbsp. tomato paste

Make a thin, light roux with the oil and flour in a pot. Add chopped onion, garlic, parsley, celery leaf and sliced carrots. Stir well, add a couple of liters of warm and simmer for half an hour. Press this through a food mill, add more water, peas, potatoes and tomato paste. Simmer until potatoes are cooked and serve with fried or toasted bread.

Vegetable Soup

3-4 carrots
green peas
small head of cabbage
2-3 tomatoes
2 potatoes
20 dag green beans
salt and pepper
3 tbsp. olive oil
1 tbsp. flour

Slice all of the vegetables and put into a pot with 2 liters of water. Bring to the boil, reduce heat and season with salt. When the vegetables are cooked, make a roux from the oil and flour with a little pepper and stir it into the broth. Serve with fried bread or croutons.

Cauliflower Soup

1 cauliflower
3 tbsp. oil
1 tbsp. flour
salt and pepper
1 potato or 15 dag rice
1 tsp. tomato paste
parsley

Clean the cauliflower and cut into small pieces. Simmer half of this in water until tender, then press through a food mill and set aside. Make a roux from oil and flour in the pot and fry the remaining cauliflower therein, then add cold water and the pureed cauliflower, bring to a slow simmer and season with salt and pepper. Add small diced potatoes or rice, tomato paste and chopped parsley and simmer until tender, adding water to the broth as needed for desired consistency.

Tomato Soup

6-8 meaty tomatoes
4 tbsp. oil
chopped onion, parsley and celery leaf
1 clove of garlic, chopped
1 sugar cube
2 tbsp. olive oil
1 tbsp. flour
salt and pepper
15 dag rice
grated hard cheese

Wash, peel, seed and chop the tomatoes, then sauté them in olive oil with the chopped onion, garlic, celery leaf and parsley. Sauté on low heat for half an hour, then add one and a half liters of water and press through a food mill. Make a roux of flour, oil, salt and pepper, then stir this into the broth and add the rice and sugar. Simmer until the rice is tender, serve with a little grated cheese. This soup is excellent with the addition of dumplings or gnocchi.

Brussels Sprout Soup

½ kg young Brussels sprouts
4 tbsp. olive oil
2 tbsp. flour
salt and pepper
2 eggs

Wash the sprouts well and cut them in half. Bring them to a boil in plenty of water, then season with salt and cook until very tender. Make a roux from the oil and flour in a separate skillet, and stir a little of the broth into this. Mix it in with the rest of the soup and add pepper. Enrich the soup just before serving with two beaten egg yolks. Serve with twice-baked toasts and a little toasted cumin seed.

Potato Soup

50 dag potatoes
½ bay leaf
5 tbsp. olive oil
2 dag flour
1 small onion
a few leaves of marjoram

Peel the potatoes, cut them into small cubes and boil them in plenty of salted water with the bay leaf. Make a dark roux from the flour and oil and add this to the broth with chopped onion and a few leaves of marjoram. Serve with fried croutons.

Panada (Bread Soup)

1 liter of water
2 bay leaves
2 hard bread rolls
salt and pepper
5 tbsp. olive oil

Boil water with the bay leaves, add the bread rolls cut into large pieces, salt, peppercorns and 5 tbsp. oil. Let the soup boil a few times, then allow to rest a few minutes and serve.

Zucchini and Rice Soup

50 dag young zucchini
5 tbsp. olive oil
½ onion
2 cloves of garlic
parsley
salt and pepper
1 tsp. tomato paste or some tomato juice
25 dag rice

Slice the onion thinly and lightly brown in the olive oil. Add sliced zucchini, chopped garlic and parsley, stir well and allow to simmer. When the juices begin to build in the pot, add plenty of water and bring to a low boil. Add salt, pepper and tomato paste, or a bit of tomato juice. Once the zucchini is tender, add well washed rice and stir continuously, adding water as needed until rice is cooked. You can serve this with a bit of grated hard cheese.

Tomato and Rice Soup

30 dag tomato
3 tbsp. oil
small onion
celery and parsley
2 cloves of garlic
salt and pepper
30-40 dag rice

Wash and dice the tomatoes. Heat 3 tbsp. oil, add finely chopped onion, parsley, celery, garlic, salt, pepper and diced tomatoes. Cook on a low flame for one hour, then put the mixture through a food mill or sieve and return to the pot. Add well washed rice and water as needed, stirring until cooked. This is a wonderful summer soup.

Spinach and Rice Soup

50 dag baby spinach
3 tbsp. olive oil
2 cloves of garlic
parsley
salt and pepper
40 dag rice

Boil the baby spinach in water, then finely chop it and press through a food mill. Set the spinach and its broth aside. In a dry pot, heat chopped garlic and parsley in the oil and season with salt and pepper. Toast the rice in this, then add the spinach and its broth, plus some more water. Simmer and stir until cooked, adding water and seasoning as needed.

SEAFOOD SOUPS

Fish soup is a central element of Dalmatian cuisine, and there are as many varieties as there are fish in the sea. Fishermen are known to add limpets or a stone from the sea to the cooking pot to enhance flavor and mineral content. Since poaching is considered the best method for preparing fish in the region, the liquid is always reserved, enhanced and served as soup. The fish itself would often become the second course, or simply served in large pieces in the broth.

In the case of the latter, the dish is colorfully known as *riba na lešo,* or 'fish, corpse style', with the word *leš* meaning 'corpse'. This colloquial reference suggests the plight of a sailor or fisherman floating lifelessly in the sea after failing to get back into his boat.

On the isle of Hvar, poached fish in broth is known as *gregada* when potatoes are added. Alternately, the meat can be removed from the bones after cooking and added back to the broth. Nearly any fish can be used, but generally it is hake, scorpion fish, grouper and other fish with white flesh.

Fish Soup

1 kg fish (grouper, monkfish, eel, etc.)
½ dL olive oil
20 dag carrots
1 celery root
2 parsley roots
1 small onion
2 cloves of garlic
2 bay leaves
black pepper
salt

Clean the fish of its innards and gills. Rinse well. Cut it into portion sized pieces. Always keep and cook the head to give the soup a rich flavor. Fry chopped onions in the bottom of the pot with a little oil, then add the fish, peeled and sliced vegetables, chopped garlic, bay leaf and peppercorns. Cover with water and bring to a gentle boil. Reduce the heat to a low simmer, add olive oil and cook for a half hour. When the fish is cooked, remove it all from the pot and set aside on a plate with a bit of the broth. Strain the broth, reserving the vegetables. Return the broth to the pot and season with salt to taste. You can add rice to the broth and cook for another 10 minutes if desired. Put pieces of fish and vegetables into bowls and cover with broth.

Stone Soup

pumice stones from the sea
sea water

When subsistence fishermen caught no fish, they were known to cook pumice stones from the sea in sea water. These porous stones contain protein from plankton and are high in minerals. When the broth is sufficiently cooked, it is poured over slices of bread in a bowl. You can certainly enhance the broth by adding soup vegetables and herbs to the pot.

Clam Soup

7 tbsp. olive oil
3 cloves of garlic
parsley
1 kg little neck clams
½ tbsp. flour
pepper

Put 4 tbsp. of olive oil, chopped garlic and parsley and clams in a wide, shallow pot. Cover tightly and heat over a medium high flame. When the shells have opened and the meat is cooked, clean the meat from the shells. In a new pot make a roux from 3 tbsp. of oil, flour and pepper. Add the clam meat and juices to this. Boil the shells in a liter of water for half hour, then add this broth to the meat and juices and stir well. Garnish with lemon juice and chopped parsley and serve with fried bread.

Crab Soup

20 small crabs
4 tbsp. olive oil
½ tbsp. flour
salt and pepper
25 dag peas or green beans
parsley

Cook about 20 small crabs in boiling water. Remove all of the meat and set aside on a plate. Crush the shells and simmer in a liter of water for about 30 minutes. Make a roux from the olive oil and flour in a new pot, add the crab meat, then strain in the broth from the cooked shells. Add the peas or beans and simmer gently for 20 minutes, season with salt and pepper. Stir in chopped parsley and serve.

Rice in Cod Broth

4 tbsp. olive oil
1 small onion
25 dag rice
salt and pepper
1 tsp. tomato paste
plenty of cod broth

Grate the onions and fry them in the olive oil. Stir in dry, washed rice and toast for a for minutes. Pour a bit of the cod broth over this, season with salt and pepper and stir in the tomato paste. When mixed well stir in the remaining broth and simmer until the rice is cooked.

Frog Soup

50 dag frog legs
3 tablespoons oil
parsley
1 clove of garlic
nutmeg
1 tsp. flour
salt and pepper
25 dag peas
tomato juice

Lightly fry chopped garlic and parsley in oil. Add frog legs, a little grated nutmeg, flour, salt and pepper. Sauté until the meat begins to cook, then add water, peas and a little tomato juice. Simmer gently for 20 minutes, then serve.

SOUP ADDITIONS

Semolina

2 tbsp. fat
4 tbsp. semolina
1 egg

Heat the fat in a saucepan and toast the semolina in it, stirring continuously until you have a nice dark golden color. Stir in a bit of cold water to prevent clumps, then strain in the hot broth of your choosing. Simmer gently for 15 minutes, stirring occasionally. Enrich the soup with beaten egg yolk before serving.

Soup Crumbs

½ kg white flour
1 tbsp. bread starter or active dry yeast
1/8 L water

Mix the yeast into the water. If you are using dry packaged yeast, you will need to dissolve a tsp. of sugar into the water before adding the yeast. Sift the flour into the water mix well into a firm dough and allow to rise. When risen add a little more flour and knead. Repeat this 3 times. By the third time, the dough should be quite firm and dry. Grate the dough into small crumbs and cook in beef or other broth.

Cancarela

2 eggs
6 dag flour
1 tsp. grated cheese

Beat the eggs with the cheese in a bowl with a spout, adding the flour a little at a time. The dough should be thick but fluid. Pour into a pot of simmering pot of soup without stirring. Bring to the boil, then remove from heat and serve.

Flan for Soup

4 eggs
salt
cup of milk
cup of cold broth

Separate the yolks and whites. Beat the egg yolks with a little salt, milk and cold broth. Pour this mixture into a lightly oiled small loaf pan. Put the pan into a skillet with a water bath to the level of the flan batter, and simmer for 10-15 minutes. Allow to cool, then cut into cubes and serve in soup.

Četvorinice

1 tbsp. fat
2 eggs
1/8 L milk
flour as needed
½ tsp. baking powder

Separate the eggs. Mix 1 tbsp. of cold fat, egg yolks, milk and flour as needed. Add baking powder and very well beaten egg whites. Mix well. This mixture should have the consistency of thin pancake batter. Heat a bit of fat in an oven-safe baking dish, pour in the batter and bake in the oven. Allow to cool after baking, then cut into cubes. When serving, put the četvorinice into the bowl, then pour hot soup over them.

Liver Četvorinice

4 dag fat
2 eggs
15 dag minced veal liver
1 dry bread roll
1 tbsp. breadcrumbs
salt and pepper

Soak the bread roll in milk and drain. Separate the eggs. Mix the fat, 2 egg yolks, minced veal liver, the soaked roll and bread crumbs. Beat the egg whites very well, then add them to the mixture with salt and pepper. Heat a bit of fat in an oven-safe baking dish, pour in the mixture and bake in the oven. Allow to cool after baking, then cut into cubes and serve with beef broth.

Palačinke (Crêpes) for Soup

1 egg
1 dL milk
1 tbsp. oil
5 dag flour

Mix all of the ingredients well and whisk until smooth. Ladle the batter in hot fat in a skillet and fry on both sides. Allow to cool, then roll them up and cut into thin strips. Serve in hot soup.

Filled Dumplings

PASTRY
10 dag flour
1 egg
lukewarm water

FILLING
2 dag fat
1 onion
15 dag finely minced meat
parsley
salt and pepper
1 egg

To make the filling, brown grated onion in the fat, then add the meat, chopped parsley, salt, pepper and a beaten egg. Allow to cool while you make the pastry.

Make your dough from the flour, egg and water, knead well, roll out thinly and cut into squares. Put a small amount of filling in the center of each square, brush the ends with egg and fold into triangle ravioli, making certain there is no air inside. Allow them to dry for a half hour. Boil in broth for around 15 minutes and serve with grated cheese.

Bread Dumplings

3 dag fat
2 eggs
parsley
salt and pepper
10 dag bread
8 dag bread crumbs

Soak the bread in milk and drain. Mix it in a bowl with the fat, 1 egg yolk, 1 whole egg, a bit of chopped parsley, salt, pepper and bread crumbs. Mix well and form into small balls. Cook in hot soup for 10 minutes and serve with grated cheese.

Bread Njoki

10 dag old bread
3 dag semolina
parsley
salt

Put the cubed bread and semolina in a bowl and pour enough boiling water to soak well. Allow to cool, then mix well with the hands, add finely chopped parsley and a pinch of salt. Knead well and form into njoki (gnocchi). Cook in boiling salted water and drain. Serve in a meat soup or sauce.

Simple Makaruni

1 kg white flour
6 eggs

Mix a stiff dough dough from the flour and eggs. Knead well, roll out a thin sheet and cut into desired shapes. You can cook these in separate water, drain and then add to soup, or add them to hot, simmering soup in the final minutes of cooking so that they take up the flavors.

Potato Dumplings for Soup

25 dag potatoes
1 egg
½ tbsp. fat
pinch of salt
10-15 dag of flour

Boil the potatoes whole until cooked, then peel off the skins and crush in a bowl. Mix and knead a dough from these along with the egg, fat, salt and flour. Form small dumplings and fry until golden in fat or oil, then serve in hot soup.

V. VEGETABLES AND ACCOMPANIMENTS

The variety of dishes made from fresh vegetables in Dalmatia is overwhelmingly grand. The recipes in this section can be served as side dishes with a full meal, but given the tendency in the region to eat smaller meals comprising many vegetables, many of them will stand alone or with soup as a light repast unto themselves.

Blitva

Swiss chard
potatoes
salt
olive oil
garlic

Wash the chard well and cut into large pieces. Peel and large dice the potatoes, then boil them in plenty of salted boiling water in a deep pot. When the potatoes are half cooked, add the chard. Cover, reduce the heat to low and simmer for approximately 15 minutes. When the potatoes are fork tender, drain off the cooking water (Reserve this cooking water for soup or other cooking, as it is high in vitamins!). Gently stir the potatoes and chard together, slightly mashing some of the potatoes. Add plenty of olive oil and chopped garlic, season with salt to taste and stir well. Cover again and allow to rest for a few minutes before serving.

Blitva with Tomatoes

1 kg Swiss chard
6 tbsp. olive oil
1 small onion
4 tomatoes
4 cloves of garlic
parsley
salt and pepper

Peel the tomatoes, remove their seeds and dice them. Heat the olive oil in a saucepan, add chopped onion and garlic, tomatoes and a little parsley, salt and pepper. Cook for half an hour, or until it begins to thicken. thicken. Separately cook the chard in boiling water until tender. Drain well, then mix with the tomato sauce.

Wild Greens

wild greens
(dandelion, thyme, poppy, wild onion, fennel, goat's beard)
salt
olive oil
vinegar and lemon juice

Wash the greens and cook in salted water. Drain, then drizzle with hot olive oil, vinegar and lemon juice. Serve with hard boiled eggs.

Endive

endive
olive oil
vinegar
eggs

Separate the endive leaves and cook in boiling water until just tender. While still hot, season with olive oil, then allow to cool. Drizzle with vinegar and serve with hard boiled eggs. Endive is high in iron, and therefore recommended for the anemic.

Wild Asparagus

wild asparagus
salt
olive oil
vinegar

Wild asparagus are in season in April and May. Wash them well, then boil in salted water for 15 minutes. Drain, cool and season with olive oil and vinegar. Serve with hard boiled eggs as an appetizer or dinner accompaniment.

Cabbage

1 kg cabbage
salt and pepper
olive oil
4 cloves of garlic

Wash the cabbage or kale well, chop and cook in boiling, salted water until tender. Drain, season with oil and pepper and add finely chopped garlic. Serve with grilled or fried fish.

Green Beans

green beans
salt and pepper
olive oil
garlic
a little vinegar
potato

Cut off the tips of the green beans, wash and cook in boiling salted water until just tender. Drain well, then drizzle olive oil and sprinkle some pepper and finely chopped garlic to taste. If you eat them cold season again with olive oil and vinegar. If desired, you may cook sliced potatoes with the beans.

Mashed Potatoes with Horseradish

50 dag potatoes
1 horseradish root
5 tbsp. vegetable oil
2 tbsp. red wine vinegar
salt
3-4 cloves of garlic
parsley

Peel and boil the potatoes. Grate the horseradish root and mix in a bowl with oil, vinegar, parsley, finely chopped garlic and salt to taste. Add the hot cooked potatoes and mash well. Serve with stewed meat or fish.

Fisherman's Potatoes

50 dag potatoes
3 tbsp. olive oil
garlic
parsley
salt and pepper

Peel, wash and cut the potatoes into rounds. Oil a saucepan, arrange the potatoes in layers and sprinkle with chopped garlic and parsley, then season with salt and pepper. Cover the potatoes with water and simmer on low heat until tender.

Potato Croquettes

50 dag cooked, mashed potatoes
1 tbsp. oil
salt
1 egg
15 dag flour
parsley

Mix the mashed potatoes well in a bowl with oil, salt, egg and flour. Roll the dough into a long sausage shape and slice into little nuggets. Fry in hot fat until golden brown. If you wish, you can dip in beaten egg and bread crumbs for a crisp, textured crust. Serve with meat or game in a rich sauce and garnish with parsley.

Noodles with Cabbage

50 dag short, flat noodles
50 dag cabbage
4 tbsp. oil
1 tbsp. fatty broth or water
1 tbsp. tomato paste
salt and pepper

Prepare basic pasta dough as described in the section on pasta. Roll out thin and flat, and cut into small squares. Boil in salted water, drain well and season. Grate the cabbage and fry it in the oil, adding a little broth or water until tender. Add the tomato paste and simmer gently until the cabbage is very tender, then sprinkle with salt and pepper, add the cooked noodles and stir together.

Braised Sauerkraut

1 kg shredded sauerkraut
3 tbsp. fat
10 dag onion
some smoked sausage, pork or pig's feet
10 dag smoked bacon
6 cloves of garlic
parsley
1 tbsp. tomato paste

Wash the sauerkraut in two changes of water and drain. Fry chopped onion in the fat until browned, then add the sauerkraut. Stir and continue to fry, adding a little broth in small quantities from time to time to prevent burning. Add diluted tomato paste, smoked sausage, pork or pig's feet, plus a paste of minced bacon, garlic and parsley. Stir together well and simmer on a very low flame for two and a half hours, adding a little broth or water as needed. This tastes better every time it is reheated!

Stewed Vegetables

½ head cabbage
2 kohlrabi
4 carrots
2 potatoes
1 tbsp. fat, or 4 tbsp. olive oil
small onion
3 cloves of garlic
parsley
1 tbsp. tomato paste
salt and pepper

Grate the cabbage, dice the kohlrabi, carrots and potatoes. Fry chopped onion in the fat or oil, add chopped garlic and parsley, then add the grated and diced vegetables. Fry on a medium low flame until the water has evaporated. Dilute the tomato paste with water or broth and stir into the vegetables. Season with salt and pepper and simmer for an hour.

Leeks

1 kg leeks
broth
1 tbsp. fat
breadcrumbs
a little vinegar
a little onion
potato
oil
salt and pepper

Wash the leeks, slice into rings and put into a saucepan. Cover with broth and simmer. In a separate skillet, fry chopped onion, diced potatoes and breadcrumbs in fat, then add to the simmering leeks. Pour in a little vinegar, stir well, cover and simmer for a half hour. Season with salt and pepper.

Stewed Peas

1 kg young peas
6 tbsp. olive oil
1 onion
parsley
salt and pepper
1 tbsp. tomato paste
4 cloves of garlic

Clean young peas from their pods. Chop the onion finely and lightly brown in the olive oil. Add the peas and sauté for a few minutes, then add chopped garlic and parsley, salt, pepper, tomato paste and a bit of water or broth. Simmer gently for approximately fifteen minutes.

Stewed Peppers

4 green peppers
salt
vinegar
5 tbsp. oil
4 cloves of garlic
parsley

Wash the peppers, remove the seeds, stems and membranes and cut into strips. Season with salt, put them on a plate and put a weighted plate on top for 15 minutes. Press out the liquid, coat with a few splashes of vinegar and leave for an hour. Lightly fry chopped garlic and parsley in oil, add the peppers, cover and simmer on a low flame until tender, adding water or broth as needed. Serve with chicken or stewed lamb.

Stewed Carrots

50 dag carrots
4 tbsp. oil
1 sugar cube
1 tbsp. parsley
salt and pepper
1 tbsp. flour
1 egg

Wash, peel and slice the carrots. Heat the oil in a pan and add the sugar cube, then the carrots and chopped parsley, salt and pepper. Cover and simmer on a low flame, adding a little water as needed. Before serving, stir in a raw egg yolk and plenty of chopped parsley.

Sour Carrots

½ kg carrots
1 tbsp. fat
3 cloves of garlic
salt
a few tbsp. vinegar
parsley

Wash, peel and slice the carrots. Lightly fry chopped garlic in the fat, then add the carrots and a bit of broth and salt. Simmer on a low flame until cooked, then add some vinegar or lemon juice and chopped parsley.

Stewed Tomatoes

1/8 liter olive oil
1 onion
6 cloves of garlic
parsley
1 kg tomatoes
salt and pepper

Fry chopped onion, garlic and parsley in the olive oil. Peel, seed and slice the tomatoes and add them to the pan. Season with salt and pepper and simmer without stirring on a very low flame for two hours until most of the water has evaporated. This is best in summertime with cold meats.

Stewed Cauliflower

1 cauliflower
1 tbsp. tomato paste
salt

Wash cauliflower, slice into rosettes and put into a pan with hot fat. Sauté, season with salt, then add tomato paste diluted in a bit of water. Simmer until tender.

Stewed Eggplant

3 eggplants
6 meaty tomatoes
4 tbsp. oil
3 cloves of garlic
parsley
salt and pepper

Peel the eggplants and cut them into small cubes. Wash, peel, seed and slice the tomatoes. Lightly fry chopped garlic and parsley in oil, add the eggplant and tomatoes, cover and simmer until tender. Season with salt and pepper.

Eggplant with Peppers

6 eggplants
6 peppers
4 tbsp. oil
6 cloves of garlic
2 tbsp. bread crumbs
2 tomatoes
parsley

Cut the eggplant into cubes and leave them in salted water for half an hour, then drain. Lightly fry chopped garlic, add the eggplant and fry until tender. Slice the peppers into strips and add them to the pot with breadcrumbs, peeled and sliced tomatoes and a little chopped parsley. Cover and simmer until all is tender.

Stuffed Eggplant

4 eggplants
3-4 tomatoes
4 tbsp. oil
1 red onion
a little garlic and parsley
salt and pepper
a few salted anchovies

Wash the eggplants, prick holes in them with a fork and leave in salted water for half an hour. Slice them in half lengthwise, scoop out the middles and chop finely. Peel and chop the tomatoes. Lightly fry chopped onion in oil until golden, then add the finely chopped eggplant and tomatoes, chopped garlic and parsley, salt and pepper.

Simmer until most of the juice has cooked out, then mix in finely chopped anchovies and chill for a while. Put the mixture into the scooped eggplant halves and put them into an oiled baking pan. Bake in a hot oven, turning them often to prevent burning on the bottom.

Fried Eggplant

4 eggplants
flour
salt

Cut an eggplant into thin slices, season with salt and leave for a while. Rinse them, dust with flour and fry in plenty of oil.

Eggplant Ajvar

4 large eggplants
salt and pepper
a few tbsp. oil
a little garlic

Wash and peel the eggplants and cook them whole in salted water to become soft. Cut them in half and leave to drain for a while. Press them through a food mill, add salt and pepper, olive oil, finely chopped garlic and mash together well. Serve with stewed beef.

Eggplant with Potatoes and Tomatoes

8 eggplants
6 tbsp. olive oil
1 onion
8 large potatoes
8 large tomatoes
a little garlic and parsley
salt and pepper

Prick the eggplants with a fork and soak in salted water for a while, then peel and cut into slices with potatoes and tomatoes. Heat the olive oil in a wide pan and layer the vegetables in it with the tomatoes on the bottom, sprinkling each layer with salt, pepper, chopped garlic and parsley. Cover with water, bring to a boil, then reduce the flame and simmer for an hour.

Artichokes

75 dag young artichokes
4 tbsp. oil
breadcrumbs
garlic and Parsley
salt and pepper

Wash the artichokes and slice lengthwise into pieces. Toss in a bowl with oil, breadcrumbs, salt, pepper, chopped garlic and parsley so that the artichoke is well coated. Put into a saucepan, cover with water and simmer until tender.

Artichokes in Oil

12 artichokes (or 20 small)
dry white wine
vinegar
2 lemons
12 bay leaves
2-3 cloves
oregano
parsley
black peppercorns
olive oil

Clean the artichokes and cut off their stems. If they are too big, cut them into quarters. Put into a pot and cover with water with some lemon juice added so that they do not darken. Add half a liter of wine, half a cup of vinegar, cloves and salt and simmer for 20 minutes. Drain well and leave to dry on a cotton cloth overnight.

Put the artichokes into jars, cover with oil and add to each jar a bay leaf, some oregano, a few peppercorns and chopped parsley. Seal the jars and store in a dark place for at least a week before serving.

Dubrovnik Cheese Pudding

10 dag butter
8 dag plain flour
7 dag grated cheese
¼ liter of milk
pepper
nutmeg
4 eggs

Melt the butter in a pan on low heat. Stir in the flour, grated cheese, milk, pepper and grated nutmeg and stir until it begins to thicken. Remove from the heat and cool. Separate the eggs and beat the whites to a stiff foam. Mix the raw egg yolks into the sauce, then stir in the foamed whites. Pour the mixture into an oiled bowl, baking dish or mold and steam gently in a water bath or over a pot of simmering water for one hour until firm. Once cooked, serve covered with spicy stewed fowl.

Spinach Pudding

40 dag spinach
5 grams butter
3 eggs
parsley
10 dag boiled ham
1 large bread roll
milk
3 tbsp. sour cream
salt and pepper
grated cheese

Break up the bread, soak in milk, then drain. Cook the spinach in water, drain well and press through a food mill. Blend softened butter with egg yolks, spinach and bread, chopped parsley, sour cream, salt, pepper and minced ham. Beat the egg whites to a foam, then stir into the mixture. Pour into an oiled form and steam in a water bath. Remove from the form when it has set and cooled a little. Serve as an appetizer or light meal with fried sausages.

Meat Pudding

½ kg ground veal or pork
12 small potatoes
salt and pepper
3-4 eggs
3 dL cream or milk

Parboil the potatoes, peel and cut them into thin slices. Layer the potatoes and ground meat in an appropriately sized, oiled mold, sprinkling each layer with salt and pepper. Beat the eggs with cream or milk, then pour the mixture over the meat and potatoes and steam in a water bath for one hour.

Zucchini Fritters

3-4 medium zucchini
2 eggs
10 tbsp. flour
milk
parsley
6 cloves of garlic
Salt and pepper

Mix the eggs, flour and milk into a batter. Grate the zucchini and mix it into the batter with chopped parsley, garlic, salt and pepper. Drop little spoonfuls into hot oil and fry on both sides. Serve as a side dish.

Eggplant Casserole

3-4 eggplants
salt and pepper
2 eggs
flour
1 red onion
30 dag minced beef or mutton
2 dL milk

Wash the eggplant and cut into thin slices lengthwise. Lightly salt the slices and leave them for half an hour to remove the bitterness. Rinse and coat with flour, then fry the slices in fat or oil. In a separate pan brown finely chopped onion with minced meat, salt and pepper. Arrange the eggplant and meat mixture in alternating layers in a greased baking dish. Beat the eggs with milk, pour over the casserole and bake.

Stuffed Onion

onion
ground veal
eggs
salt and pepper

Peel several onions and boil them in salted water. Drain, scoop out the middle. Lightly brown the veal, drain and cool. Mix with beaten eggs and pepper, then fill the onions with this. Bake in a greased baking dish, serve with tomato sauce.

Stuffed Peppers

8 bell peppers
25 dag ground beef
25 dag ground veal or lamb
25 dag ground pork
parsley
6 cloves of garlic
1 red onion
1 egg
oil
tomato juice
salt and pepper

Slice the tops off the peppers and remove the seeds. Mix the ground meat with chopped garlic and parsley. Lightly fry the meat in oil with chopped onion. Drain and cool well, season with salt and pepper and mix in the egg. Fill the peppers with the mixture, arrange them upright in an oiled baking dish and bake. When they are half cooked, pour the tomato juice into the dish and continue baking until tender. Serve with the tomato juice poured over the pepper. These are wonderful with mashed potatoes.

Đuveč

10 dag fat
10 dag onions
25 dag rice
8 bell peppers
1 kg tomatoes
½ kg pork leg
salt and pepper

Wash the rice well. Slice the tomatoes and peppers. Slice the onions into rings and fry them in hot fat. Stir in the tomatoes, peppers and rice and fry a little. Mix in diced pork, season with salt and pepper and pour into a glass baking dish. Bake in a medium oven until the meat is roasted and the vegetables are tender.

VI. PASTA, RICE AND DUMPLINGS

The love for pasta in Dalmatia is testament to Italy's influence on the region. We will train our focus on some essential favorites. Many dishes in other sections of this book call for serving with pasta, as you will see.

Great rewards await those who master the art of making pasta from scratch. Simpler, more versatile noodle varieties are often prepared in large batches well in advance and dried for later use. If you possess a pasta rolling and cutting machine or an electric extruder, by all means take advantage of the convenience. But the skills you will gain from practice with a rolling pin, knife and a wooden spoon handle will travel with you freely and widely.

Weights given refer to the dry weight of pasta, but dried homemade pasta will still have a higher water content than factory made noodles. Use common sense, good judgement and the learning that comes with experimentation when adjusting quantities.

Pasta should always be cooked *al dente.* This means completely cooked, yet still slightly resistant to the bite. When your pasta achieves this hallowed state, remove it from the boiling water and rinse it with cold water immediately to stop the cooking.

Basic Pastry for Noodles

½ kg flour
4 eggs
2 tbsp. water

Sift the flour onto a clean, dry surface and make a well in the middle of the pile. Put the eggs into the center of the flour, then fork the flour into the eggs and add the water. Mix well and knead by hand until you have a smooth, firm dough. Divide the dough into two pieces, and roll each of them out quite thinly, keeping the second piece cover with a towel so that it doesn't dry while you roll the first. Allow the rolled sheets of pasta to dry for an hour or two, then cut into noodles of the desired thickness and length, or cut squares and fill as with ravioli. Cook the pasta in salted boiling water until it rises to the surface. Drain and rinse with cold water. Add sauces and seasonings as desired, or serve in soup or stew.

Noodles with Pršut

50 dag pasta of any shape
2 tbsp. fat
10 ounces prosciutto
grated cheese

Cook pasta, drain and rinse in cold water. Chop the prosciutto into small cubes and fry in the fat. Stir this into the pasta and serve with grated cheese.

Spinach Noodles

50 dag baby spinach
2 cloves of garlic
20 dag flour
1 egg

Crush the garlic and simmer with the spinach in water until just cooked, drain well and press through a food mill. While it is still warm, knead this puree with flour and egg into a firm dough. Roll and shape as desired, then allow to dry for a bit. Cook well as with any other pasta, drain and rinse. Serve with a veal or other meat sauce.

Kaštelanski Makaruni

1 kg flour
4 eggs or 6 egg yolks
6 dag butter
salt
sherry
grated cheese
nutmeg
lemon
fried sausages, or braised meat or poultry stew

Mix a dough from the flour, eggs or egg yolks, butter and salt. Add the sherry to this and knead well. Cover the dough with a damp cloth on a cutting board and allow to rest for 12 hours. Knead again and divide into pieces. Keep the dough you are not working under a damp cloth.

Roll out a piece of dough thinly and cut into squares of about 5 cm. Now you will need a narrow piece of wooden rod, such as a wooden spoon handle. Make sure it is dry, and dust it with some flour. Roll each square around the end of the rod to form cylinders, starting on a corner so that the ends are pointed rather than flat. Roll tightly to preserve this shape and slide the noodle from the end of the rod. Repeat until you have used all of the dough.

Spread the makaruni on a board and allow to dry. Cook in salted boiling water and drain well. Serve with a stew, or fried sausages with a sauce. Sprinkle with grated cheese, ground nutmeg and a little chopped lemon peel. This style of noodle is very rich and flavorful.

Dubrovnik Style Noodles

For Dubrovnik style pasta: Make pasta dough, roll out thin and cut into long strips about 3 cm wide, and 30 cm in length. Roll the entire strip lengthwise around a thin rod, applying pressure to seal into a 30 cm long tube. Slide the tube from the rod and cut into 3 noodles. Continue in this fashion until you have used all the dough, spread the tubular noodles on a board to dry. Cook in boiling salted water, drain and rinse.

Dubrovački Šporki

50 dag juicy beef shoulder
12 dag fat
1 onion
1 tbsp. of tomato paste
beef or vegetable broth
grated cheese

Cut the beef into bite sized pieces. Heat the fat in a saucepan and brown finely chopped onion therein. Add the beef and brown this well also, stirring constantly until all the juice has run from the meat. Stir in the tomato paste, cover, reduce heat and simmer for up to 4 hours until tender, adding broth as needed when the juices have cooked out. Serve this over boiled pasta or gnocchi with grated cheese.

Dry-Cooked Pasta

1 kg pasta
4-5 tomatoes
chopped celery root
parsley
5-6 carrots
1 pepper
2 onions
4 tbsp. oil or fat
salt and pepper

Put chopped tomatoes, celery root, parsley, grated carrots, chopped peppers and 1 onion into a saucepan with dry pasta. Simmer on low heat for 1-2 hours, strain the juice and reserve. Grate the other onion and brown in a skillet with the fat. Add the strained juices, salt and pepper. Pour this over the pasta and serve.

Špaget with Sardines

50 dag spaghetti
6 tbsp. olive oil
1 onion
3-4 salted sardines (or 6-8 salted anchovies)
1 tbsp. of tomato paste

Boil the pasta in 3 liters of water until cooked. Drain and rinse in cold water. Heat the olive oil and add chopped onion and chopped sardines. Add 4 tbsp. of water with the tomato paste and stir well. Simmer and stir for 10 minutes, add the spaghetti, mix well and serve hot.

Špaget with Clams

400 g clams
1 dL olive oil
3 cloves garlic
chopped parsley leaf
1 dL white wine
40 dag of spaghetti
salt and pepper
fish or shellfish broth

Cook the spaghetti, rinse in cold water and drain well. Heat the oil in a deep, wide saucepan and fry the clams therein. When they begin to open, add chopped garlic, parsley and white wine. When the wine begins to simmer, season with salt and pepper. Add the spaghetti and toss well, add broth and simmer until the pasta is again hot. This will serve four people.

RICE AND RISOTTOS

When we differentiate between rice and risotto dishes, we speak of the consistency. Both may benefit from the addition of meat, fish poultry and vegetables, and can be cooked in broth. Risottos, however, are thick, brothy and creamy - like a rice stew - while the goal in preparing other rice dishes is to add only as much liquid as the grains will absorb. Somewhere between these two there are 'rice in broth' dishes that are like risottos, only the broth remains essentially liquid. When you bear these differences in mind you will have success with rice and risottos.

To achieve the thick consistency for risottos it will be helpful to use a short grain rice with a high starch content, such as Arborio, Carnaroli, Baldo or Roma. Rice should still always be washed of excess starch and drained before cooking.

Festive Rice of Poljica

2-3 green cabbages
celery root
onions
carrots
1½ kg beef
1 kg dry pork
1 kg lamb
1-2 chickens with giblets
10 grams of fat
liver
fresh peas
rice
1 tbsp. tomato paste or a few fresh tomatoes
horseradish
pickled shallots, peppers and cucumbers

This dish is served on special occasions in Poljica. All kinds of meat except game and fish are used. This recipe is intended for 16-20 people, and you may increase or decrease the quantity of meat as needed.

In plenty of cold water, cook chopped celery root, onion, carrots, cabbage, and beef. After half an hour, add strips of dried pork or prosciutto, and after an hour add the lamb. Sooner or later, you will add the chickens cut into pieces. An older chicken should be added sooner. Allow this all to simmer, adding water as needed.

Heat some fat in a separate pot and brown some more grated onion with finely chopped liver and chicken gizzards. Add the peas to this. Pour in some broth into which has been dissolved a spoon of tomato paste, or chopped fresh tomatoes which have been stewed and reduced. When this is all well fried, add the rice and sautee for a bit, then add plenty of broth in which the meats have cooked. Stir this over a medium flame, adding broth a little at a time until the rice is cooked. Put the cooked rice on large serving plates, cut the meats into pieces and arrange on top. Serve with grated horseradish and pickles from shallots, cucumbers and hot peppers.

Rizi-Bizi

green peas
4 tbsp. fat
1 onion
parsley
tomato juice or paste
rice
grated cheese
vegetable broth

Remove the peas from their pods and wash well. Brown some grated onion in the fat, add the peas and some chopped parsley and fry for a bit. Add a little tomato juice or paste, cover and simmer for a fewe minutes. Then add washed rice and stir, adding broth little by little until the rice is cooked. Sprinkle with grated cheese and serve.

Rice with Liver

1 lamb liver, or ½ kg veal liver
2 tbsp. fat
1 small onion
nutmeg
20-30 dag rice
grated cheese
meat broth

Remove all of the plumbing from the liver, wash and chop into small pieces. Chop the onion ond fry it in the fat. When onions are tender, add the liver and a bit of nutmeg. Allow to simmer on a low heat for 20 minutes, then add washed rice and broth and simmer until the rice is cooked. You will wnat it a little saucy rather than dry, so add broth as needed. Serve with grated cheese.

Rice in Broth with Luganiga

beef or chicken broth
5-6 dag rice per person
fresh sausages (luganige)

This is a favorite for festive winter luncheons. The recipe for luganiga can be found in the chapter on meats. Simmer the rice in plenty of excellent broth so that you have a rich soup consistency when it is cooked. Fry two sausages per person, slice them into large pieces and add them to the cooked rice. Stir well and simmer for a few minutes before serving with grated cheese.

Rice with Cabbage in Broth

4 tbsp. olive oil
1 small onion
parsley
2 cloves of garlic
50 dag cabbage
1 tbsp. tomato paste or juice
25 dag rice
salt and pepper

Brown the finely chopped onion in the oil, add a few leaves of parsley, chopped garlic and finely chopped cabbage. When the cabbage turns completely golden, add some broth, tomato paste or concentrate, salt and pepper. Simmer until very tender, then add washed rice, stir well and add broth as needed until the rice is cooked.

Rice with Cauliflower

1 cauliflower
3 tbsp. fat
1 onion
broth
fresh tomato juice or a teaspoon of tomato paste
salt and pepper
30 dag rice
grated cheese

Wash and chop a small cauliflower, then brown with chopped onion in fat. Add broth and tomato paste or juice, simmering until the cauliflower is very tender. Add washed rice and a bit of salt. Simmer and stir, adding broth as needed until the rice is cooked. Sprinkle with grated cheese before serving.

Rice with Potatoes

4 tbsp. olive oil
1 onion
a few medium potatoes
salt and pepper
broth
1 tbsp. tomato paste
30 dag rice
grated cheese

Fry chopped onion in the olive oil, then add some small diced potatoes. Season with salt and pepper and continue to fry. Dissolve some tomato paste in broth and add this to the saucepan. When the potatoes become very tender, add washed rice and simmer, stirring and adding broth as needed until the rice is cooked. Sprinkle with grated cheese before serving.

Rice Croquettes

20 dag rice
2 dag fat
20 dag flour
2 eggs
salt
10 dag bread crumbs
¼ liter vegetable oil
parsley

Cook the rice and drain it. When it has cooled, mix it in a bowl with one of the eggs, fat, flour and a little salt. Form into small croquettes, coat each with flour, then beaten egg and bread crumbs. Fry in hot oil. Sprinkle with chopped parsley and serve with green salad.

Beef Risotto with Cabbage

30 dag beef
1 head cabbage
3 tbsp. fat
1 onion
broth
1 tbsp. tomato paste
salt and pepper
40 dag grated cheese
rice

Remove the core of the cabbage, then cut it into very thin strips. Brown the onion in fat, then add the cabbage and cook until golden. Add broth in which you have dissolved some tomato paste, then simmer until the cabbage is nearly dissolved. Season with salt and pepper. Add beef that has been cut into small cubes, add broth and simmer until the meat is tender. Add washed rice and broth, stirring all the while and adding more broth as needed until the rice is just tender. Stir in grated cheese. Risotto should have the consistency of very thick stew. Sprinkle with more grated cheese before serving.

Chicken Risotto

3 L water
root vegetables for soup
1-2 hens or 1 large cock
5 tbsp. olive oil
onion
a few tomatoes
1 tbsp. tomato paste
1 teacup of rice per person
salt and pepper
a few slices of butter
4 tbsp. grated cheese
a little nutmeg

Cook the whole fowl in water with soup vegetables. When half cooked, remove all of the meat from the bones, break into moderately large pieces and set aside. Fry chopped onion in the olive oil, then add the chicken meat and saute until it has a nice color. Stir in the tomato concentrate and a little bit of broth. Wash one cup of rice per person, stir it into the meat and allow to toast in the pan for a bit. Season with salt and pepper, stirring constantly, add broth a little at a time until the rice is cooked. Stir in grated cheese, butter and a little ground nutmeg. The rice should not be dry, but brothy and thick. Sprinkle with cheese when serving.

Lamb Risotto

1 kg lamb from the leg
2 tbsp. fat
1 large onion
tomato juice
salt and pepper
broth
8 dag dry smoked bacon
2 cloves garlic
parsley
40 dag rice
grated cheese
grated nutmeg

Remove the lamb meat from the bone and cut into pieces. Fry the chopped onion in the fat until golden, then add the meat and fry to a nice color. Add a bit of tomato juice and season with salt and pepper. When the meat has simmered for a bit, make a nice chopped paste of bacon, garlic and parsley and stir this into the meat. Simmer for a few minutes, the add the rice and stir it into the mixture well for a few minutes. Add broth as needed and cook until the rice is tender, thick and brothy. Sprinkle with grated cheese and a little nutmeg when serving.

Quail Risotto

2 quail
2 tbsp. fat
1 onion
salt and pepper
broth
1 tbsp. tomato paste
40 dag rice
grated cheese

Clean the quail, wash well and allow to air dry a bit, then cut each into four pieces. Fry the chopped onion in the fat until you have a nice color, then add the quail and fry for a bit. Season with salt and pepper and stir in some tomato paste dissolved in broth. Allow this to cook for a few mintues, then ad rice and broth, stirring constantly and adding broth as needed until the rice is cooked. When you have a nice brothy rice, stir in a good handful of grated cheese. Allow to rest for a few minutes before serving.

River Eel Risotto

1 river eel
4 tbsp. olive oil
½ onion
parsley
2-3 cloves of garlic
salt and pepper
1 tbsp. tomato paste
40 dag rice
wine vinegar or lemon juice

Chop the onion finely and fry in the oil, then add pieces of eel that have been cleared well of bones. Add a bit of chopped parsley, chopped garlic, salt, pepper and a teaspoon of tomato paste. Allow this all to brown for a bit, add a little water and continue simmer for a few minutes. Then add the washed rice and some hot water and simmer, stirring all the while. Add water as needed until the rice is cooked. Taste the rice and adjust the seasoning to taste. Add a little vinegar or lemon juice and more parsley. This is a very rich dish.

Squid Risotto

50 dag squid
8 tbsp. olive oil
small onion
3 cloves of garlic
parsley
salt and pepper
2 tbsp. red wine vinegar
30-40 dag rice

Clean the squids, removing the innards and quill bone. Take care not to burst the ink sacs, and set them aside. Rinse the squid well. In a deep skillet fry chopped onion in teh olive oil. When the onion begins to take on a nice color, add chopped garlic and parsley, salt, pepper, squid and vinegar. Saute this over high heat, and when it begins to take a nice color again, add the ink. Stir well, reduce the heat and allow to simmer for 15 minutes, adding a little lukewarm water, or white wine. When the meat is tender, add washed rice. Stir continually, adding hot water a little at a time until the rice is cooked and the squid is very tender. Raise the heat for a minute, then cut the flame, add a little vinegar and olive oil to taste and allow to rest for 10-15 minutes.

Prawn Risotto

large prawns
4 tbsp. olive oil
a little garlic
parsley
tomato juice
40 dag rice
salt and pepper
1 tbsp. vinegar
grated cheese

Clean and peel the shrimp, and cut off their heads. Cook the shells and heads in a pot of water to make a broth. Strain liquid and reserve.

Heat the olive oil in a deep, wide pan, add some chopped garlic and parsley. When the garlic is lightly browned, add the cleaned shrimp tails and enough tomato juice to cover them. Bring this to a high simmer and let the juice thicken a little. Add the washed rice and stir continually, gradually adding shrimp broth until the rice is cooked. Add salt, pepper and a spoon of vinegar, stir in some grated cheese and serve.

Crab Risotto

1 kg crabs
5 tbsp. olive oil
3 cloves of garlic
parsley
salt and pepper
tomato paste
40 dag rice

Boil the crabs until cooked. Remove from the water, pluck out all of the meat and set aside. Return the shells to the water and cook for a while to get a nice broth. Strain the broth through a sieve and set aside. You will want to end up with about 1½ liters of broth.

Lightly fry some chopped garlic and parsley in olive oil, then add the crab meat, and salt and pepper if needed. Add a bit of tomato paste and stir well. Stir in the rice and a bit of broth, and continue adding broth as it is absorbed, stirring all the while until the rice is cooked. Allow a few minutes to rest before serving.

Cuttlefish Black Risotto

20 dag cuttlefish
20 dag mussels
20 dag squid
1 large onion
2 dL olive oil
1 tbsp tomato paste
1 dL of white wine
salt and pepper
4 cloves of garlic
parsley
30 dag rice
grated cheese
cuttlefish ink
fish broth

Clean all of the squid and cuttlefish, and reserve the ink sacs (you may use packaged ink if necessary). Cut these fish into pieces. Fry the chopped onions lightly in olive oil, add the mussels, squid and cuttlefish, garlic and tomato paste. Cover and simmer on medium heat. When the mussels have opened remove them, take out the meat and return it to the pan. Add white wine, rice and the ink from the squid and cuttlefish. Stir well, add broth and proceed as with other risottos until the rice is cooked, occasionally adding a bit of grated cheese to thicken. You may include other shellfish such as clams and scallops if desired. Sprinkle with grated cheese when serving

Limpet Risotto

1 kg limpets
5 tbsp. olive oil
4 cloves of garlic
parsley
salt and pepper
40 dag rice

Wash the limpets well to remove sand and grit, but leave any seaweed. Lightly fry chopped garlic and parsley, then add the limpets, salt and pepper and continue to cook on low heat until the meat is tender. Remove the meat from the shells, then return it to the pan. Cook the shells separately in a liter of water to make a broth, then strain this broth. Add the rice to the limpet meat and garlic and fry it a little before adding broth gradually and cooking to completion.

Clam Risotto

1 kg little neck clams
5 tbsp. olive oil
4 cloves of garlic
parsley
salt and pepper
40 dag rice

Wash little neck clams well to remove sand and grit. Lightly fry chopped garlic and parsley, then add the clams, salt and pepper and continue to cook on low heat until the clams open. Remove the meat from the shells, then return it to the pan. Cook the shells seperately in water to make a liter of broth, and strain this broth. Add the rice to the clams and fry it a little before adding broth gradually and cooking to completion. Serve thick and sprinkle with chopped parsley.

Mussel Risotto of Vranjic

1 kg of mussels
6 tbsp. olive oil
a little garlic
parsley
25 dag rice
1 tsp. tomato concentrate
grated cheese

Wash the mussels well to remove sand and grit. Lightly fry chopped garlic and parsley in oil, then add the mussels, salt and pepper and continue to cook on low heat until the shells open. Remove the meat from the shells, then return it to the pan. Cook the shells seperately in water to make a liter of broth, and strain this broth. Add the rice to the meat and fry it a little before adding broth gradually and cooking to completion. Serve thick and sprinkle with chopped parsley.

Fan Mussel Risotto

fan mussels
1/8 liter olive oil
1 onion
4 cloves of garlic
parsley
fresh tomato juice
salt and pepper
2 tbsp. red wine vinegar
40 dag rice
white wine

Carefully open the shells and take out the meat. Remove the dark entrails from the mussels, as this is very bitter. Rinse the meat well of any sand and debris, keeping an eye out for the occasional worm. If you are not confident in your ability to properly clean fan mussels, ask your fishmonger to do it for you. Slice the meat into pieces.

Fry chopped onion, garlic and parsley lightly, then add the meat. Cook this until the moisture is gone, then add tomato juice and water to cover, season with salt and pepper, cover the saucepan and simmer on a low flame for 1 hour. Then pour in the vinegar and white wine, stir in the rice and proceed with broth or water until the rice is cooked, as with other risotttos.

DUMPLINGS

Palenta

25 dag corn flour
a little oil or fat
1 onion

Boil the corn flour in water for 15 minutes, then simmer on low heat for 45 minutes, stirring and adding water as needed. You should end up with a very thick porridge. Allow this to cool completely, then scoop dumplings of the desired size with a spoon. Arrange on a plate and sprinkle some onions fried in fat, then cover with stew. Fish brudet is best!

Corn and Potato Dumplings

50 dag potatoes
25 dag corn flour
oil or fat

Boil the corn flour as described above. Cook potatoes separately, mash them very well and stir into the hot porridge witha little fat. Allow to cool, make firm dumplings and serve with stew or brudet.

Njoki

1 kg potatoes
1-2 eggs
a pinch of salt
1 tablespoon fat or butter
10 dag flour

Boil the potatoes in their jackets until cooked, then rinse and peel while still hot. Press them through a food mill or potato ricer, put the mash on a board and mix in the eggs, salt, fat or butter, and enough flour to create a firm dough. Knead the dough well and roll out by hand in the form of a long sausage. Cut into walnut sized pieces, then press a fork across each dumpling to make indentations. Cook in boiling water until they rise to the surface. Carefully drain them well and serve with a sauce, stew or goulash and grated cheese. This is a favorite of Dalmatians, especially with beef pašticada.

Baked Njoki

1 kg potatoes
25 dag flour
10 dag grated cheese
15 dag butter
4 eggs
salt and pepper
a little nutmeg
stew or meat sauce

Cook the potatoes in their jackets, peel and salt lightly. Push through a food mill or potato ricer. Add the flour, half the grated cheese, butter and eggs, a little grated nutmeg and pepper. Mix and knead so that the dough is uniform. Boil some water and drop in large dumplings with a spoon. Cook and drain them well.

Place the njoki on an ovenproof serving plate, then ladle some ragout or meat sauce, sprinkle with plenty of grated cheese and top with a few slices of butter. Bake in a hot oven for a few minutes until the cheese melts and takes on a golden crust, then serve.

Semolina Dumplings

5 dag semolina
2 tablespoons oil
1 egg
salt
parsley
grated cheese

Beat the egg with the oil and a little salt, then add semolina and a little finely chopped parsley. Mix well, spoon dumplings into simmering broth and cook for about 10 minutes. For softer dumplings, separate the white from the egg, mix the yolk with all of the other ingredients, then beat the egg white to a foam and mix into the dough just before cooking. Serve in the broth with grated cheese.

Spinach Dumplings

15 dag spinach
5 dag butter
2 eggs
15 dag flour
2 dL milk
salt

Mix softened butter, eggs, flour and milk, then add spinach which has been cooked and put through a food mill. Mix well, then spoon dumplings into boiling water or broth. Drain well, toss with melted butter and serve with stew.

VII. SALADS

Salads are an important part of the Dalmatian diet, valued for their nutritional content and the crisp balance they lend to meals featuring cooked dishes. Raw vegetable salads can even be a main dish for the midday meal, especially when the bountiful variety of the summer garden allows for the composition of elaborate medleys. A summer meal of grilled fish with a bright, acidic vegetable salad has few equals.

Always wash vegetables thoroughly and pat them dry before preparation. They should be seasoned with the highest quality olive oil and vinegar available, and salt, pepper and other spices should be very finely ground. White pepper is better than black for these dishes.

Cabbage Salad

1 head of cabbage
salt and pepper
oil
vinegar

Remove the outer leaves and core of the cabbage. Wash well and grate the cabbage finely. Season with salt and allow it to cure for half an hour. Press the liquid from the cabbage, add pepper, oil and vinegar and mix well. Serve with roast meat.

Pickled Cabbage Salad

1 kg pickled cabbage (sauerkraut)
oil
pepper

Wash the cabbage well, slice into short, thin strips if it was pickled whole. Add oil and pepper and mix well. As simple as it is, this is a very healthy salad. It was typically enjoyed by the peasantry with hot palenta.

Tomato Salad

a few meaty tomatoes
salt and pepper
4 tbsp. oil
parsley and garlic

Wash the tomatoes well, slice thinly and arrange in a single layer on a plate. Season with salt and pour over some olive oil, then sprinkle some pepper. Tomatoes provide their own acidity, so you shouldn't use vinegar. Garnish to taste with chopped garlic and parsley.

Cucumber Salad

cucumbers
oil
salt and pepper
vinegar
2-3 cloves of garlic

Peel the cucumbers then slice in half lengthwise and scoop the seeds from the middle. Slice into pieces and toss in a bowl with the remaining ingredients. Allow to rest for a half hour before serving.

Beet Salad

4 beets
2 tbsp. red wine vinegar
3 tbsp. oil
a little cumin
1 tbsp. lemon juice

Wash, peel and grate the beets. Toss with vinegar in a bowl and leave it for an hour. Drain well and season oil, ground cumin and lemon juice. This is a very healthy salad.

Carrot Salad

4-5 carrots
salt
juice of 1 lemon
2 tbsp. oil

Wash and scrub the carrots well, grate and mix in a boil with salt and lemon juice. Allow this to cure for half an hour, then add oil and mix well.

Eggplant Salad

4 eggplants
15 dag grated cheese
olive oil
salt
white pepper

Wash eggplant, cut lengthwise in slices and dry them well. Sprinkle with salt and allow to cure for half an hour to draw out the bitterness. Rinse and dry again. Season with a little salt and pepper, then fry or grill on both sides on both sides. Arrange on a plate, sprinkle grated cheese and olive oil liberally. This is even more delicious when it has cooled.

Celery Root Salad

2 celery roots
handful of celery leaf
a couple of celery stalks
salt
3 tbsp. oil
a little vinegar or lemon

Wash the roots, leaves and stalks of celery. Peel the skin from the roots, then cut all into thin strips. Season with salt, mix well and allow to rest for an hour. Drain the liquid that accumulates, pour in the oil and vinegar or lemon juice. This is delicious with cold fowl.

Potato Salad with Anchovy

50 dag potatoes
1 onion
1 apple
2 salted anchovies
salt and pepper
3 tbsp. oil
2 tbsp. red wine vinegar

Boil the potatoes, peel and slice them. Mix in a large bowl with finely chopped onion, diced apple, chopped anchovies, pepper, oil and vinegar. Season to taste with salt, chill and serve.

Mixed Vegetable Salad

15 dag of dry beans
2 potatoes
3 beets
½ cauliflower
capers
pickles, boiled eggs

Dressing:
2 egg yolks
½ cup olive oil
½ lemon

Boil the beans until tender. In a separate pot boil potatoes, beets and cauliflower. Peel the potatoes and beets and slice. Break the cauliflower into small rosettes. Mix the cooked beans and vegetables. For the dressing, blend two egg yolks with the juice of half a lemon. Whisk vigorously while gradually drizzling in the oil. Pour this over the vegetables, add some capers and mix well. Arrange on a serving dish and garnish with pickles and boiled eggs.

.

Lentil Salad

25-30 dag lentils
2 apples
1 onion
2 salted anchovies
salt and pepper
3-4 tbsp. olive oil
2 tbsp. red wine vinegar

Cook, drain and cool the lentils, then mix with diced apples and onion, finely chopped anchovies, vinegar, oil, and salt and pepper to taste. Serve with roast meat.

Spicy Cauliflower Salad

1 small cauliflower
2 large carrots
2 horseradish roots
1 apple
lemon juice
salt, oil
1 tbsp. spicy mustard

Wash and chop the cauliflower, carrots and apples. Grate or chop the horseradish root. Mix well in a bowl with oil, the juice of one lemon and a tbsp. of spicy mustard. Serve with roast meat.

White Bean Salad

white beans
olive oil
salt and pepper
2 onions
vinegar

Cook and drain the beans. Mix with oil, thinly sliced onion, salt and pepper while warm. Add vinegar when cooled.

Egg Salad

6 boiled eggs
3 stalks of celery with leaves
3 carrots
1 large onion
parsley
vinegar or lemon juice
olive oil
salt and pepper

Dice the celery, onions and carrots. Chop the parsley and celery leaf. Mix all in a bowl with salt and pepper and leave it for 15 minutes. Add olive oil and vinegar or lemon juice. Peel and dice the eggs and toss them gently with the vegetables.

VIII. FISH AND SEAFOOD

"A fish must swim three times: in the sea, in olive oil, and in wine." – Dalmatian proverb

The importance of fish and seafood in the Dalmatian diet cannot be overstated, and the length of this section will show that. The bounty and variety of edible species in the Adriatic Sea is the backbone of this grand old cuisine, and the people's fondness for fish is among the primary causes for their robust health. Indeed, a diet that relies chiefly on the flesh of aquatic creatures as a protein source is a foundation for long life. When combined with the antioxidant properties of fresh olive oil, the fatty oils of fish are excellent for a healthy heart and circulation.

When preparing a meal with several fish courses, shellfish and oysters should be served first after the soup. Crabs, risottos, poached fish and stews should be brought next, and superior quality fried or grilled fish would be served as the final fish course. Cold and marinated fish, pâtés and seafood salads should be served as appetizers or early intermediary courses. Always keep olive oil, wine vinegar, white pepper and lemon slices at the table when serving fish.

Particular attention should be given to fish preparation, from procurement to cooking. As much as they are tasty and nutritious, so can fish be harmful if not absolutely fresh and well maintained. When buying fresh fish, the gills should be bright red and the eyes clear and shiny. Also bear in mind that most species are better at certain times of the year, and this depends on spawning habits. Medium-sized fish are preferred, as a larger, older fish will have drier, tougher meat. Small, young fish have the sweetest meat, but you must be wary of tiny bones.

It is best to buy fish early in the morning, as soon as the market opens, but buy it last before making your way home if you have far to travel in warm conditions. Fish should be cleaned immediately, then prepared as soon as possible. Cleaning should not be put off until evening, as decomposition of the organs and blood can ruin the quality and flavor of the flesh. Modern refrigeration affords us a means of staving off this natural process for a little while, but you should not take this as license to be lazy. The succulence of your meal will reflect the care and expedience with which you have dispatched preparation duties.

Clean the fish by first scraping the scales from head to tail, then remove the gills and cut along the belly. The entrails should be removed very carefully so that organs are not ruptured, and do not release bile, waste and other unsavory substances to taint the meat. The skin around the belly should be removed. Take special care when cleaning fish to avoid pricking your skin with sharp bones and teeth, as some species contain irritating bacteriae, or even poisonous substances. Therefore, shears and pliers reserved specifically for removing bones and fins are recommended items for your cutlery drawer.

Freshwater fish are lighter and easier to digest. Trout is especially recommended for those with digestive disorders, and larger trout are often salted and smoked with delicious results. River mullets, porgies and eels are higher in nutritional value among freshwater species, but not recommended for the sick, nor for those with delicate constitutions.

Cold fish preparations are especially suited to the hot Dalmatian summers. Serve with lemon juice or vinegar, or prepare them in a marinade (*savura* in the coastal dialects) to keep fish viable and flavorful for several days. Grill, roast or lightly fry the fish, then immerse it in the marinade for several hours prior to serving.

Roasted fish are best served with salads and greens. If you opt to fry, roll the fish in flour an hour in advance and allow it to dry. This will make a nice crust when the fish is fried.

The Adriatic Sea is home to a remarkably diverse array of fish species, and most of them eventually find their way into a Dalmatian kitchen. It would require another book to go into full detail on all of the aquatic creatures harvested from the sea and rivers, but I can certainly list a few, along with their respective seasons and common preparations.

SEA FISH

Hake (oslić) is among the most frequently eaten fish in Dalmatia. It is fished year round, but especially bountiful and delicious from October to March. It is best poached or fried, and can be dried and smoked for winter.

Sardines (srdela) are a very common fish of the Adriatic, and excellent grilled. They are available all year round, but most plentiful in the summer. In addition to grilling, they can be fried, poached, baked or marinated. They are often pickled and jarred, or dry salt cured in great quantities for use throughout the year.

Common Pandora (arbun) are a type of bream available throughout the year, but most plentiful in spring. They are excellent for soup and brudet.

Garrick (bilizma, lica bjelica) is fished all year. The flesh is quite tasty, especially in summer and autumn. Garrick is generally poached, stewed or fried.

Red Scorpion Fish (škarpina) is a common fish of the Adriatic, very succulent and delicious all year. The typical preparation is stewing in a brudet, but they can be poached as well.

Anchovy (inćun) is fished from spring to winter, with the season slowing down at the end of summer. When preserved in a salt cure, it becomes a staple ingredient of the Dalmatian kitchen, adding flavor and richness to many dishes. It is also fried or added to stews when fresh.

Bogue (bukva) is fished throughout the year. It is typically grilled.

Flathead Grey Mullet (cipal) is a very common fish, mostly caught in spring and autumn when it is tastiest. It is often fried or grilled.

Smelt (gavun) This small net fish is the common food of sailors and fishermen, commonly fried, or roasted on skewers whole.

Red Mullets (trlja) are best from September to April, and typically grilled or fried. They are prized for their juiciness and pronounced flavor. Red mullets are especially delicious.

Rays (golub, raža) are bountiful all year, and best poached or fried.

Monkfish (grdobina) is bountiful year round, and prized for its distinctive flavor and nutritional value. The skin is always removed, and it is usually poached, stewed or fried.

Garfish (iglica) is caught in fall and winter. Good for frying or in stews.

Swordfish (sabljarka) is best roasted or fried.

Flounder (ivorak) is bountiful in autumn and winter. The moist flesh is often fried or featured in stews, but it is also delicious coated with bread crumbs and baked.

Moray Eel (murina) is considered a delicacy, especially on the island of Korčula, whence come the oldest traditional recipes for it. It hides between rocks and must be hunted very carefully, as it is especially aggressive and has a poisonous bite. Its blood is also toxic, but the poison is rendered harmless with thorough cooking.

Conger Eel (ugor) is quite common, and its meat is flavorful and juicy. It can be fried or stewed, or roasted on a spit next to a wood fire.

John Dory (kovač) is bountiful and delicious all year round. It is best poached, fried or stewed.

Gilt-Head Bream (orada) has excellent meat and is among the most prized Adriatic fish. It is usually grilled.

Saddled Sea Bream (ušata) is bountiful year round and is usually made into stews, but can also be grilled.

Sole (list) is considered one of the highest quality fish, and most flavorful in spring and autumn. It is usually coated with bread crumbs and fried, but can also be baked or grilled very carefully.

Sea Bass (lubin, brancin) is caught near the mouths of rivers throughout the year, but is especially tasty in summer and autumn. It is most commonly grilled, but can be poached or roasted.

Peacock Wrasse (lumbrak) is an excellent fish with tender flesh, usually fried, but also poached.

Cat Shark (mačka) is a small species of shark. It is not widely prized, but can be fried, poached or stewed.

Red Porgy (salpa) is a species of bream fished in summer and autumn. The flesh is very tasty, and usually poached or grilled.

Shark (morski pas) is caught all year, but best in autumn and winter. It can be poached or sliced crosswise and fried, always without the skin.

Greater Weever (pauk) is very tasty poached or stewed. Special care must be given to removing the fins and head before cleaning so that bones do not prick the fingers, as the sting can cause serious illness.

Bonito (palamida) is plentiful in spring, summer and autumn. The flesh is juicier than that of tuna, and not as dark. It is best grilled or stewed, or preserved in marinades.

Tuna (tunj) is fished with nets in spring, summer and early autumn. It is prepared in a wide variety of ways, and preserves well in brines and marinades.

Angel Shark (sklat) is considered better than other sharks for eating, and is very nutritious. It is usually poached.

Mackerel (skuša) is best in spring and summer. It is best grilled, roasted on skewers, stewed, or cut into pieces and fried. It is excellent served in cold marinades in summer, and preserves well for winter.

Horse Mackerel. (šnjur, šarun) is common, and plentiful in summer. Roast it carefully so that it does not become dry, and serve with oil and vinegar.

Chub Mackerel (lokarda) is excellent in the spring and summer. It is prepared in the same variety of methods as ordinary mackerel.

Sprat (srdelica, papalina) is a smaller sardine. They are especially tasty fried or in stews.

Pickerel (modrak) is caught mostly in the spring and summer. It is a very common fish, and best fried or grilled.

Whiting (mol) has moist, tender, nutritious flesh, and there are many varieties. Poach it with onions or fry.

Dentex (zubatac) is caught all year, but mostly in summer and autumn. It is less common than other fish, but highly regarded. Poach, fry or stew dentex, or roast it on skewers for a real treat.

Octopus (hobotnica) is boiled for cold salads, and is especially tasty when roasted with potatoes and wine. It can be dried and kept over winter, then rehydrated and fried.

Musky Octopus (muzgavac) are nearly always boiled. They are excellent for seafood salads.

Cuttlefish (sipa) are excellent poached or stewed. Smaller cuttlefish are generally used for risotto, or you can mince the meat and make it into croquettes.

Greater Squid (lignjun) are good for stewing, frying, or stuffed and roasted.

Lesser Squid (lignja) are prized for their particularly sweet flavor. Excellent for risotto, frying or poaching.

CRUSTACEANS

Crustaceans should always be prepared live. While the meat is very moist and delicious, it is slightly more difficult to digest. It is suggested to tie the tails of lobsters to a stick before cooking them so that they cannot jump out of the pot.

Lobster (hlap) is best in winter. It is excellent boiled or grilled, and can made into lovely cold salads.

Spiny Lobster (jastog) has no claws and is generally more tender than ordinary lobster. It is best in winter, and, as with other lobsters, is better when it is no heavier than one kilogram. Boil and enjoy with a piquant mayonnaise sauce.

Crabs (rak) are harvested in winter and spring, and have the most meat during the full moon. They are excellent boiled with spices, grilled, or made into soups.

Langoustines (škampi) are typically grilled, stewed in the buzara style or boiled like crabs. They can also be added to risotto.

Prawns (kozica) are excellent grilled, fried, stewed as buzara or made into risotto.

SHELLFISH

All species of shellfish are best in winter and early spring.

Fan Mussels (loščura) are very tasty stewed in the buzara style, or in pastas and risotto.

Oysters (kamenica, oštriga) are best in winter. You must be certain that they came from pristine water. Eat raw with lemon juice, or roast over coals.

Mussels (dagnja) are usually prepared as buzara, but can be roasted over coals or served in pasta or risotto.

Scallops (jakopska kapica) should be grilled, roasted or pan seared.

Noah's Ark Mussels (kunjke, mušule) are best roasted or in risotto.

Limpets (prilipak, lupara) are best made into soup or risotto.

Cockles (kapica prugasta) make a wonderful soup, but can also be stewed as buzara or added to risotto.

Date Shell Mussels (prstaci) are best stewed as buzara or added to risotto. Date shell mussels must be hammered out of the coastal rocks in which they grow. This causes damage to the natural ecosystem, and so the harvest of date shell mussels is outlawed in Croatia.

Clams (kučice) are excellent prepared as soups and buzara, or added to risotto and pasta.

FRESHWATER FISH

Trout (pastrva) is considered the tastiest freshwater fish. It is excellent year round. It is commonly poached, fried or smoked.

Perch (smuđ) is highly prized for its delicate flesh. Poach or fry.

Crayfish (slatkovodni rak) are found in rivers and creeks, and can be prepared in various ways. They are delicious from May to October.

Freshwater Eel (jegulja) are most bountiful in autumn when migrating to the sea to spawn. They are among the oiliest of fish, hence quite flavorful. They can be stewed, deep fried, grilled or made into risottos, but the favored method of preparation is roasting on skewers before a wood fire.

Frogs (žabe) are good all year, and tastiest in the fall. Frog meat is easy to digest, and is generally fried or stewed. The famous brudet of Neretva contains whole frogs.

PRESERVING FISH

Many varieties of fish are salted and dried for long storage. The simplest way is to cover the bottom of a bucket with salt, arrange the fish thereupon and sprinkle liberally with salt again. Cover with a piece of wood, apply a load of large stones on top and allow to cure for 48 hours. Then remove the fish pieces, rinse and hang to dry in an airy place. In summer, dry in the sun and wind. During winter the fish should be dried for two days in the wind, then smoked.

OCTOPUS

On the northern Dalmatian coast, fishermen preserve octopus by drying. The head is removed, arms are salted and stretched on thin rods or branches, then hung in a windy place until firm and dry. Store in a cool, dry place. Before cooking, you will need to wash dried octopus and soak it in warm water for an hour. Then the meat is typically fried in oil.

SHARK

The sharks typically caught in the Adriatic are smaller, usually weighing a few kilograms at most. Remove the heads, skin and innards of the shark, rinse and dry, then rub well with crushed garlic, salt and pepper. Arrange them in an earthenware bowl and cure for 2 hours, then hang out to dry in a windy place for one day. Smoke the sharks for 12 hours or so and store in a cool, dry place. When preparing, rehydrate the shark as with octopus above, then poach or fry.

MACKEREL

Remove the heads, cut the mackerel lengthwise along the belly, then remove the innards. Rinse well, open fish lengthwise so that the body lays somewhat flat. Coat liberally with sea salt and allow to cure for an hour. Secure the body open with a short twig and hang in the sun so that the inside of the fish is facing the sunlight. Once dry, store in a cool, dry place. Mackerel can then be poached or fried as needed.

TUNA

5 kg tuna
35 dag of salt
1 cup red wine vinegar
a few bay leaves
peppercorns
olive oil
capers

Tuna should be cut into large steaks. Put the tuna into a wide pot, add the salt and vinegar, then enough water to cover the fish. Cook on low heat for about 2 hours until completely cooked. Drain and allow to cool and dry on a clean board. Remove any skin, bones and blobs of cooked blood from the meat, and break into large pieces that will still fit into wide glass jars. Put the tuna into the jars with a bay leaf and a few peppercorns and capers in each. Add enough excellent olive oil to the jar to coat and cover the fish. Tie two sheets of parchment over the moith of the jar if they do not have their own lids. Store in a cool, dark place. It can be eaten cold with its oil and some lemon juice, or prepared with spaghetti.

Winter Tuna with Spaghetti

40 dag cooked spaghetti
10 dag tuna
6 tbsp. olive oil
1 onion
2 cloves of garlic
parsley
1 tbsp. tomato paste

Cut the tuna into fork-sized pieces. Fry chopped onion and garlic in olive oil, then add the tuna, chopped parsley, tomato paste and a little water. Stir together and simmer for 10-15 minutes, pour over cooked spaghetti and serve.

SARDINES AND ANCHOVIES

Large quantities of sardines and anchovies are often salt cured. Once preserved, they can be enjoyed as a cold appetizer or added to recipes for seasoning and a rich, deep flavor. Cut the fish along their bellies and remove the innards. Wash well. Sprinkle a layer of salt in a wooden bucket, add a layer of cleaned fish, sprinkle more salt and repeat until you have used all the fish. Allow to cure for several days, pouring off accumulated liquid as needed (in Roman times, this liquid would be saved and used as a condiment and ingredient called *garum*).

When the fish are completely cured, scrape the scales and remove the heads. Arrange them in a jar (you can add sliced onions, lemon and capers to the jars if desired) and pour in enough oil to cover. Tie some parchment over the mouth of the jar if it does not have a lid. These fish will keep indefinitely when covered in a cool dark place. Serve these as an appetizer with olives and capers to counter the salt content, and drizzle some fine olive oil.

Pickled Sardines

1 kg sardines
5 dag salt
1 L water
½ L white wine vinegar
15-20 peppercorns
1 onion
5-6 bay leaves
parsley leaves
lemon peel
olive oil

For each kilogram of fish, you should use 5 dekagrams of salt. Clean the fish, cut off their heads, rinse and gently pat dry. Put the water and vinegar into a pot with peppercorns, thinly sliced onion, bay leaves, a handful of parsley leaves and the chopped peel of one lemon. Bring to a gentle boil, then reduce the flame to very low, add the fish and simmer for 30-45 minutes. Remove from the heat, skim fat and debris from the surface and allow to cool in the liquid. Lay the fish out side by side on a clean board and allow to air dry overnight. Put the fish into glass jars with a few peppercorns. Pour good olive oil into the jars so that it rises one finger width above the level of the fish. Cover with lids or tie with parchment. These will keep all winter.

POACHED FISH

Start with cold water, and along with the fish add salt, peppercorns, sliced onion, parsley, lemon peel and bay leaf. Pour in two spoons of vinegar to keep the flesh firm. Once brought to the boil, reduce the heat and simmer until the fish is cooked, then remove from the flame and allow the fish to rest in the broth. Remove the fish, pour over some olive oil and sprinkle with pepper. This is indeed a simple, austere preparation, but it is considered the best way to cook fish by Dalmatians. If the odor of simmering fish is objectionable to some in the house, a small piece of charcoal added to the simmering pot will help.

Freshwater fish can also be poached in boiling water with salt, peppercorn, bay leaf and some sliced onion. Again add a few tablespoons of vinegar to the poaching broth so that the flesh remains firm. This acidity also cuts certain brackish flavors while lending its own exquisite bite. Fish cooks quickly in comparison to other flesh, so cook it gently and remove from heat as soon as it is finished. The fish is cooked when the eyes pop up white and the flesh separates easily from the bone. It is nearly always served with a generous splash of olive oil.

Poached Dentex

dentex
olive oil
onions
salt and pepper
a few peppercorns
few bay leaves
lemon
vinegar
olives and capers
parsley

Soak the fish in warm water for a few minutes to help loosen the scales, then remove scales, organs and gills. Add the fish to a pot of salted cold water with a halved onion, peppercorns and bay leaf. Simmer very slowly for about an hour. When the meat begins to come away from the bones, the fish is cooked. Carefully remove the fish from the water and set on a serving plate. Drizzle some olive oil and sprinkle a little pepper. Serve with potatoes or cauliflower, and keep lemon slices, capers, olives, parsley, olive oil and vinegar at the table to allow each guest to season to taste. Avoid other sauces and condiments, as they would ruin the taste of the fish.

Poached Sea Bass

sea bass (or bream, hake, mullet, porgy, etc.)
olive oil
lemon
boiled potatoes

Place the cleaned fish in cold salted water and bring to a simmer. Simmer slowly until cooked. Carefully remove the fish and serve with boiled potatoes (you can simmer the cooked potatoes for a few minutes in the poaching broth if desired). Drizzle with olive oil and lemon juice.

Poached Baby Squid

baby squid
salt and pepper
olive oil
lemon juice or vinegar

Clean the squid well and bring to a boil in salted cold water. Remove from heat and drain immediately once boiling, add good olive oil and pepper, then cool. Serve the cooled squid with lemon juice and vinegar.

Bakalar na Bijelo

30-40 dag dried cod
salt and pepper
1/8 L olive oil
2 cloves garlic
l kg potatoes
parsley

Soak the dried cod in water for 1-2 days, then drain and rinse. Put into a pot of cold, salted water, bring to a boil and simmer until tender. Take the cod from the broth, remove the skin and bones. Peel and slice the potatoes and cook them in the fish broth, then drain. Put the cod and potatoes into a mixing bowl with chopped parsley, garlic, salt, pepper and olive oil. Add a few tablespoons of the cod broth. Mash all of this together well and serve.

Cod in Milk

one dried cod
½ cup olive oil
½ cup butter
milk
salt and pepper

Soak the cod in water overnight until well reconstituted. Remove the fin bones, put the fish into the bottom of a pot, add the olive oil and butter and cover with milk. Cover and simmer gently for half an hour. Season with salt and pepper.

Fisherman's Cod

30-40 dag dried cod
2 dL olive oil
2 large onions
8 cloves of garlic
½ bunch of parsley
4-5 tomatoes
salt pepper
l kg potatoes

Soak the cod for 1-2 days in water. Remove the bones and fins and cut into large pieces. Put the olive oil, chopped onion and garlic, parsley, crushed tomatoes and cod into a deep, wide saucepan. Season with salt and pepper and cook on a medium flame for 20 minutes. Add peeled, sliced potatoes and water to cover, then simmer for another 30 minutes. Shake the pot rather than stirring so that the cod does not break apart. This is a very traditional dish for Christmas Eve.

Mackerel with Capers

1 kg mackerel
salt and pepper
parsley
1 onion
plenty of olive oil
juice of 2 lemons
handful of capers

Clean the fish thoroughly, rinse and put into a pot with enough cold water to cover. Add salt, a few peppercorns, parsley and chopped onion. Bring the pot to a boil, remove from the heat and leave it for 15 minutes. Drain the fish when it has cooled, remove the head and bones, then pour over plenty of olive oil and lemon juice and sprinkle with chopped capers. This is commonly prepared in the early afternoon and enjoyed at dinner

Poached Mackerel

1 kg mackerel
1 onion
black pepper
4-5 salted anchovies
2 tablespoons capers
¼ L olive oil
1 cup red wine vinegar

Clean and wash the mackerel thoroughly, then place in salted cold water with a halved onion and a few peppercorns. Once brought to the boil, reduce heat slightly and cook for another 5 minutes or so. Once cooked, drain the fish and remove the head and bones, leaving filets intact. Arrange these on a plate.

Chop the anchovies and capers very finely and fry them in the olive oil. Add the wine vinegar to this and stir well, then pour it over the fish, cover and leave it for a while. This is delicious when served cold.

Stewed Cuttlefish and Musky Octopus

cuttlefish
musky octopus
olive oil
salt and pepper
several cloves of garlic
wine vinegar

Wash and gut the octopus and cuttlefish. If the octopus is large and old, you should beat it with a mallet or rolling pin to tenderize. Simmer both in plenty of unsalted water for 2-3 hours. Drain and place in a bowl with a bit of the cooking liquid. Pour over some fine olive oil and season with salt and pepper. Serve with chopped garlic and vinegar.

Stewed Octopus

1 large octopus
olive oil
salt and pepper
several cloves of garlic
vinegar

Clean the octopus, wash and drain. Cover the bottom of a pot with olive oil and add the octopus without water. Add crushed peppercorns, cover with a lid and cook on a low flame for approximately 45 minutes. When cooked, remove, carve into pieces and arrange in a bowl. Season with salt, chopped garlic, parsley and wine vinegar to taste.

Red Mullets in Tomato Sauce

red mullets
olive oil
garlic
2 fat tomatoes, peeled and diced
1 L tomato juice
salt and pepper
a few leaves of fresh basil

Clean the fish well, then fry briefly in a little olive oil. Remove and set aside on a plate. In a deep skillet put chopped garlic, diced tomatoes and ¾ of the tomato juice, salt, pepper, a few leaves of basil and simmer gently for half an hour. Meanwhile, mix the remaining tomato juice with a few tablespoons of cold oil. Place the fish into the sauce in the pan, then pour over the cold tomato sauce. Simmer gently for another 20 minutes, adding a little water as needed to prevent scorching.

Poached Ray

1 ray
1/8 L of olive oil
1 onion
parsley
salt and pepper
lemon juice

Clean the ray well. Put it into a pot with the olive oil, thick slices of onion, chopped parsley, salt and pepper. Add enough water to cover, bring to a boil, reduce heat and simmer uncovered until the ray is tender. Arrange on a plate and serve with lemon juice.

Corned Net Fish

1 kg of small net fish (pickerel, smelt, sprat, etc.)
salt and pepper
head of garlic
olive oil

Clean the fish of their scales and guts, wash and dry. Mince plenty of garlic very finely, then crush it with plenty of salt. Coat the fish evenly with this mixture by tossing in a bowl. Arrange the fish in a dish, cover with a plate and load some weight on top. Cover this with cheese cloth or a fine strainer to prevent flies from touching the fish, then allow this to rest overnight. Wash the fish and simmer in water, or grill them. Season with olive oil, salt and pepper.

Corned Hake

1 kg hake
garlic
salt
olive oil
lemon juice

Clean and rinse the hake, rub with a paste of chopped garlic and salt. Put it into a dish, put some weight on top and cover it overnight. The next day, wash the fish well and cook it in water as with any other fish. Season with olive oil and lemon juice and serve with cooked greens.

Poached Sardines

large sardines
olive oil
bay leaf
salt and pepper
lemon juice
potatoes

Clean the sardines and simmer them in a bit of water with olive oil and bay leaf. Drain the fish, then season them with olive oil, salt, pepper and lemon juice. Serve with boiled potatoes.

Poached Tuna Belly

tuna belly
olive oil
salt and pepper
lemon juice or vinegar
piece of celery root
half of an onion
parsley
5-7 laurel leaves
a few cloves

Poach the upper part of the tuna belly in a pot of salted water with the olive oil, vinegar, onion, a bit of parsley, a few grains of pepper, and three or four bay leaves. Cook gently for one hour. When just cooked through, remove the tuna belly, drain and place on a plate. On top of the meat put two or three fresh bay leaves and a few cloves, then cover with plenty of olive oil. Allow the tuna belly to rest for 24 hours. Douse the belly with a bit of lemon juice or vinegar before serving.

Smoked Moray

smoked moray
salt
garlic
parsley
laurel
sage leaves
cabbage or kale
olive oil
a little vinegar
lemon
½ an onion

Clean the moray well. Rub with a paste of salt, chopped garlic and parsley. Stretch and secure the moray lengthwise on a stick. Hang this in the smokehouse and allow to dry in fragrant smoke. The woods of myrtle, pistachio, spruce, alder and strawberry tree are best, and you can occasionally add some bay and sage leaf to the coals. After 14 days of drying and smoking, the moray is ready to be cooked.

Cut the moray into pieces and wrap tightly in blanched cabbage or kale leaves, then arrange in a deep skillet. Add water, olive oil, wine vinegar, garlic, lemon slices, parsley, bay leaf and sliced onion in proportions appropriate to the quantity of fish. Simmer well until the fish is very tender.

CRUSTACEANS

Steamed Crabs

2 kg live crabs
¼ L water
1/8 L vinegar
a few peppercorns
a handful of salt
a few laurel leaves
1 onion
2-3 tablespoons olive oil
parsley
garlic

Wash the crabs well. Heat the water, vinegar, peppercorns, salt, bay leaves and two halves of an onion in a deep pot. When it begins to boil, add the crabs, stirring them around a few times so that they are steamed evenly. Cook them for about 15 minutes, or just until they begin to turn red. The shells will retain heat and continue to cook the meat after you drain them. Place the crabs in a large bowl after draining, add chopped garlic, parsley and olive oil. Cover the bowl and shake it around, then allow it to rest for a bit before serving.

Steamed Crabs, Sinj Style

2 kg live crab
a little red wine
plenty of garlic
10 tablespoons olive oil
salt and pepper

Wash the crabs well in several changes of water. Put the crabs in a pot with a little red wine to cover the bottom, add plenty of chopped garlic and olive oil, then season with salt and pepper. Cook covered for 10-15 minutes, stirring frequently.

Crayfish Steamed in Wine

1 kg crayfish
1 cup water
salt and pepper
parsley
glass of wine
6 tablespoons olive oil
7 cloves of garlic

Wash the crayfish and put them in a pot with water and a handful of salt. Bring to a boil. After 10 minutes of cooking, add the wine, pepper, olive oil, chopped garlic and parsley. Cook for another 5 minutes, then remove from the flame and serve.

Steamed Crabs, Skradin Style

1 kg live crabs
5 tablespoons olive oil
salt
parsley
6 cloves of garlic
cup white wine or wine vinegar

Wash the crabs well. Heat 5 tablespoons of olive oil in a deep, wide skillet and add the crabs. Fry on all sides for about 10 minutes, then add a small handful of salt chopped garlic and parsley, and the wine or vinegar. Shake well so that the crabs are evenly coated with the liquid, cook for a few more minutes, then serve.

Baked Crabs

1 kg live crabs
3 tablespoons bread crumbs
½ bunch of parsley leaves
6 cloves of garlic
salt and pepper
6 tablespoons olive oil
lettuce
boiled eggs

Wash the crabs in several changes of water. Arrange them on a baking pan and bake in a very hot oven on both sides for a few minutes. Make a cut on the top shells of the crabs from head to tail. Mix a paste from bread crumbs, finely chopped parsley and garlic, salt, pepper and olive oil. Put a little of the paste in the cut you have made, then return the crabs to the oven and bake again until a crust forms on the paste. Arrange on a bed of lettuce on a serving plate and garnish with boiled eggs. Serve as appetizers.

Fried Langoustines

Wash the langoustines well and boil or steam as in any of the above recipes. Then fry them in hot oil, drain and season with salt. Pour some olive oil and lemon juice over them and serve hot.

Škampi na Buzaru

1 kg langoustines
1 dL olive oil
1 cup white wine
½ cup tomato juice
garlic
parsley
1 tablespoon bread crumbs
salt and pepper

In a deep, wide pan, heat the olive oil. Add the langoustines and fry for a minute, then add a glass of white wine and cook a few minutes more. Add the tomato juice, salt and pepper, then shake the pan. Sprinkle with chopped garlic, parsley and bread crumbs and stir the broth. Simmer for 15 minutes. If the sauce becomes too thick, add a little water or wine.

Prawns in Green Sauce

1 kg prawns
1 lemon
1 cup olive oil
teaspoon ground mustard seed
tablespoon chopped parsley
salt and pepper

Simmer the prawns in spiced water for 15 minutes. Remove the tails and peel the meat from the shells. Mix the lemon juice, olive oil, salt, pepper, ground mustard and chopped parsley and beat well with a fork. Pour this over the tail meat in a bowl and toss well to cover. This sauce can certainly be served with other boiled or grilled fish.

Crabs in the Shell

large, meaty crabs
olive oil
salt and pepper
garlic
parsley
juice of ½ a lemon for each crab

Wash large crabs very well and boil in plenty of water until they turn bright red (about 20 minutes). Drain and cool. Remove the top shell, taking care to keep it intact. Take all of the meat from the body cavity and claws. If there are eggs, add them to the meat. Wash the shells well to remove any spongy and hairy bits. Chop the meat into pieces and mix in a bowl with olive oil, chopped garlic and parsley, lemon juice, salt and pepper. Mix this well, spoon the meat mixture back into the shells and heat on a grill over coals for 5 minutes. Serve as an appetizer.

Kotor Style Crabs

large, meaty crabs
3-4 tablespoons olive oil
1 onion
4 cloves garlic
parsley
roasted sea bass or other delicate white fish
a few peppercorns
lemon juice
grated cheese
crumbs
lettuce and radish

Clean the crabs well, scrubbing the moss form the shells. Cook in salted boiling water for 20 minutes. Remove all the meat from the shells and claws, leaving the shell intact. Wash the shells. Mix the meat in a bowl with olive oil, an onion which has been chopped and fried, cracked peppercorns, chopped garlic and parsley, and the cleaned, roasted meat of a sea bass. Add the lemon juice and some grated peel with a little bit of water and mix well. Put the mixture back into the shells, sprinkle with grated cheese and a few drops of olive oil. Bake in a hot oven for 15 minutes until it takes on a nice golden color. Serve in the shells, arranged on a serving plate on a bed of lettuce and some sliced radishes.

Lobster Salad

1 lobster
½ cup red wine vinegar
¼ L olive oil
salt and pepper
4 tablespoons white vinegar
lemon

Lobster is best when not much larger than half a kilogram, and they must be prepared live. Boiled salted water with wine vinegar in a deep pot. You can secure a small stick lengthwise at the beginning and end the tail to prevent it from jumping out of the pot. As soon as the water boils, drop the lobster into the pot. Boil for a half hour or a little longer. When cooked, remove the lobster from the water and allow to cool it down in some cold water. Remove all of the meat from the shell, tail and claws. Mix olive oil, salt, pepper and white vinegar and beat to a thick emulsion. Pour this over the lobster meat and toss before serving.

You can also blend thoroughly cooked, tender octopus meat with the lobster for this simple salad. Serve as an appetizer with baby lettuces, boiled eggs and lemon slices.

Roasted Oysters

oysters
olive oil
lemon juice
pepper

Remove the top shell of live oysters. Drizzle a little olive oil, lemon juice, salt and pepper on each one and roast on the grill over hot coals, or in a very hot oven for just no more than 5 minutes. Serve immediately.

Vranjic Mussels

1 kg mussels
parsley
garlic
crumbs
pepper
a few tablespoons of olive oil
lemon

Scrub the mussels well and remove the mossy beards. Open each shell carefully and discard the half that does not contain meat. Arrange the shells with the meat side by side in a roasting pan. Mix together chopped garlic and parsley, olive oil, bread crumbs and pepper and put a little of this mixture over the meat in the shell. Now heat some olive oil to nearly smoking in a separate pan, and pour a spoonful of this hot oil over each mussel. Bake the mussels in a hot oven for about ten minutes. Serve with lemon slices as an appetizer.

Dagnje na Buzaru

1 kg mussels or dateshell mussels
10 tbsp. olive oil
garlic
parsley
pepper
glass of white wine
bread crumbs

Wash the mussels well and remove their beards. Heat the olive oil in a wide saucepan and stir in finely chopped garlic, parsley, a few spoons of breadcrumbs and some pepper. Fry this a little, then add the mussels. Stir them around so that the fried mixture is dispersed. When the mussels begin to open, add the glass of white wine, stir well, and allow to simmer. Taste the broth and add salt and pepper if needed. You can serve them from the pot, or line the bottom of a serving bowl with toasted bread slices, pour the mussels and broth over and serve.

FISH STEWS

There are a few dishes that are emblematic of Dalmatian cuisine, and *brudet* is likely its crowning glory. Alternate regional spellings for this simple fish stew include *brodet* and *brujet*, while in Italy it is known as *brodetto*. There are countless variations of *brudet*, each featuring various types of whole or sliced fish, seafood and seasonings. The classic preparation typically begins with a base sauté of sliced onions in which the fish is first lightly seared, then removed. The sauce is then built with parsley, garlic, tomatoes and wine, and the fish is returned to this liquid to simmer gently for up to an hour. Brudet should not be stirred while the fish cooks, so that the meat does not fall apart. Once the fish is cooked and the broth is well flavored, the brudet can be gently spooned atop a starch, such as palenta dumplings. The famous cioppino of San Francisco is essentially a brudet, and was introduced there by Dalmatian and Italian sailors.

One fisherman's style of brudet is noticeably different from the typical preparation. For each kilogram of fish, you would mix together ¼ liter of olive oil, 1/8 liter of vinegar, two chopped onions, four chopped cloves of garlic and a spoonful of salt and pepper. Whisk this together into a thick emulsion in the cooking pot. Lay the cleaned fish or large fish pieces therein, add enough water to cover and bring to the boil. Cook on high heat for a few minutes, then reduce to a very low simmer and cook for about an hour, occasionally shaking the pot.

On the isle of Korčula, the brudet might begin by stewing small net fish such as smelts. When cooked, these will be crushed, the heads and bones removed, and the juices and crushed meat become the base for a brudet of larger fish. As you can imagine, this technique yields especially flavorful results.

However you will stew your fish, stew it *very slowly and gently.* Shake the pot rather than stirring. Always use the freshest fish available, and resist the temptation to embellish the sauce too much. Fresh sage leaf or chopped rosemary in very small quantity are acceptable aromatics, but bay leaf and chopped parsley should suffice on their own.

Fisherman's Brudet

fish
olive oil
onion
garlic
salt and pepper
tomatoes to taste
wine or sherry
pumice stone from the sea
sea water
bread

Fisherman's brudet is usually cooked from several kinds of fish. These are most often the smaller species that do not fetch a handsome price at market. Historically the preference was to cook the brudet in a clay pot, as it produces a stew of superior flavor.

Put olive oil, sliced onions, garlic, salt, pepper, tomatoes and fish into the pot. Cover this with cold water or, better yet, sea water. Add a glass of wine. Bring this to a simmer and cook very slowly. You can add a stone from the sea to enhance the flavor.

Kotorski Brudet

1 kg fish
¼ liter of olive oil
3 large onions
5-6 cloves of garlic
parsley
1 tablespoon flour
glass of white wine
5-6 tomatoes
2 bay leaves
pepper

Clean the fish. Fry chopped onions in the olive oil. When tey take on a nice color, add chopped garlic, a bit of chopped parsley and a spoonful of flours. Stir this well into a light roux, then add plenty of hot water, a glass of white wine, crushed tomatoes, bay leaves and a little pepper. Allow this to simmer slowly for a half hour, then add the fish and simmer for about an hour.

Eel Brudet

1 kg conger eel
2-3 tbsp. olive oil
2 onions
parsley
3-4 cloves of garlic
salt and pepper
2-3 tomatoes
vinegar

Clean the eel and wash in several changes of water, then cut into large pieces. Brown chopped onion lightly in olive oil, then add the eel and fry on all sides. Remove from the heat and add some parsley, chopped garlic, salt, pepper, chopped tomatoes, a few spoons of vinegar and enough water to cover the fish. Bring to a boil, then reduce the heat and allow to simmer gently for an hour on low heat. Eel is a very fatty fish. If there is excessive fat on the surface of the broth, skim it off. Serve with palenta dumplings and cooked greens.

Monkfish Brudet

monkfish
6 tbsp. olive oil
2 onions
4 cloves of garlic
parsley
2-3 tomatoes
1 tablespoon tomato paste
salt and pepper
vinegar

Clean the monkfish, remove the tail, fins, skin and head, and slice the meat into large pieces. Fry chopped onion in the olive oil, add chopped garlic and parsley and crushed tomatoes. Fry this for a bit, then add the fish and simmer on high heat until the fish begins to take on some color. Add water to cover, salt and pepper and simmer gently for about an hour, shaking the pot occasionally. Add a little vinegar to taste and serve with palenta.

Fisherman's River Eel

1 kg eel
6 tbsp. olive oil
6 cloves of garlic
1 onion
parsley and celery leaf
tomato
1 cup brandy
glass of red wine
salt and pepper

Clean the eel, wash it well and cut into pieces. Fry the eel on all sides in olive oil, then remove and set aside on a plate. In the same oil, brown chopped garlic and onion, add chopped parsley and celery leaf, crushed tomatoes and simmer for a bit. Add a cup of brandy and a full glass of red wine, return the eel to the pot and season with salt, pepper and vinegar. Simmer gently for about an hour.

Brudet of Moray Eel

1 kg moray eel
1/8 liter olive oil
6 cloves of garlic
parsley
baby cuttlefish or squid
onion
salt and pepper
vinegar
tomato juice

Clean the eel well and cut into pieces. Fry chopped onion, garlic and parsley in olive oil, then add the eel and other cleaned fish when the garlic just starts to brown. Season with salt and pepper, add water to cover and simmer gently for an hour. When the liquid has reduced by about half, add a teaspoon of vinegar per serving and some tomato juice. Simmer for a bit longer, shaking the pot every so often, and serve.

Brudet of Trout

1 kg nice, fat trout
8 tbsp. olive oil
2 onions
5 cloves of garlic
parsley
salt and pepper
1 tbsp. tomato paste
1-2 tbsp. red wine vinegar

Clean the trout and cut into large pieces. In a wide, shallow pot fry the sliced onion in olive oil. Add the fish, chopped garlic, parsley, salt, pepper, tomato paste and a bit of water. Bring to the boil, add 2 tbsp. of vinegar or white wine, then reduce heat and simmer gently, shaking the pot occasionally. This brudet is especially good when eaten cold.

Brudet of Mackerel

1 kg mackerel
1/8 liter olive oil
4 cloves of garlic
salt and pepper
a few tomatoes
parsley

Clean the fish and cut into large pieces. Fry chopped garlic and tomatoes, add the fish and season with salt and pepper. Add water to cover and simmer slowly for 30 minutes to an hour. Sprinkle with chopped parsley just before serving.

Brudet of Crab

1 kg crabs
50 dag potatoes
1/8 L olive oil
salt and pepper
parsley
garlic
3 tbsp. red wine vinegar

Wash the crabs well. Peel and slice the potatoes. Into the pot you will put the olive oil, crabs, salt, pepper, chopped parsley, garlic and potatoes. Bring to a boil, add the vinegar, reduce heat and simmer for 30 minutes.

Brudet of Shellfish

1 kg mussels, clams, etc.
8 tbsp olive oil
6 cloves of garlic
½ bunch of parsley
pepper
½ cup of white wine

Wash the shellfish well in several changes of water to remove sediment and debris. Lightly fry chopped garlic, parsley and pepper in olive oil. Quickly add the shellfish and some wine, and simmer for 10-15 minutes.

Brudet of Tuna

1 kg tuna
6 tbsp olive oil
1 onion
garlic
parsley
1 kg tomatoes
salt

Cut the tuna into thick steaks, season with salt and fry on both sides int he olive oil. Remove from the pot and set aside. Add chopped onion and fry for a bit, then add chopped garlic, parsley, and tomatoes sliced into thick rounds. Place the tuna steaks on top of the tomatoes and simmer very gently for an hour. Season with salt and serve.

Mackerel with Tomatoes

1 kg mackerel
salt and pepper
¼ L olive oil
6 cloves of garlic
parsley
50 dag tomato

Clean and rinse the fish, then pat dry with a clean cloth. Season with salt and pepper, coat well with olive oil and bake whole in a hot oven until nearly cooked. In a wide pan simmer the olive oil, chopped tomatoes, garlic and parsley. Remove the filets from the mackerel lengthwise and be certain to get out all of the bones. Lay these in the sauce and simmer for another 15 minutes.

Tuna with Tomatoes

50 dag tuna
6 tbsp olive oil
a little garlic
salt and pepper
30 dag tomatoes
parsley

Lightly fry chopped garlic in olive oil in a deep, wide pan. Add the tuna, chopped tomatoes and parsley and simmer on a low heat. Season with salt and pepper, adding hot water or vegtable broth as desired to increase the amount of sauce.

MARINATED FISH

Savura of Assorted Fish

3 kg fish
½ L olive oil
¾ L vinegar
¾ L water
4 sugarcubes
1 head of garlic
4 bay leaves
10 peppercorns
salt
fresh lemon peel
1 sprig of rosemary

Preheat the olive oil in a pot, then add vinegar, water, sugarcubes, chopped garlic, bay leaves, peppercorns, chopped lemon zest, rosemary sprig, and salt if needed. Bring to a boil, then simmer for 15 minutes. Allow to cool. Grill or roast the whole, cleaned fish. Allow them to cool, then arrange them in a deep dish and pour the marinade over them. Leave for eight hours before serving. The fish will keep for several days.

Savura of Mackerel

1 kg mackerel
flour
¼ L olive oil
1/8 L red wine vinegar
1/8 L water
parsley leaves
rosemary leaves
6 peppercorns
salt
lemon

Clean the fish and remove the heads. Wash well and pat dry with a towel. Season with salt, coat with flour and allow them to sit for a half hour, then fry in hot oil and arrange them in a dish. Boil the water, vinegar, olive oil, parsley leaves and peppercorns for ten minutes, then pour over the fish. Store in a cool place, and serve with lemon wedges.

Savura of Sardines

1 kg sardines
¼ L olive oil
1/8 L red wine vinegar
6 cloves of garlic
parsley
grated peel of one lemon
1 sugarcube
rosemary leaves
salt and pepper

Remove the innards and heads of fresh sardines, wash them well fresh and pat dry with a towel. Season with salt and pepper and fry in hot oil. Arrange in a deep dish. Boil the vinegar for a few minutes with the chopped garlic, parsley, lemon peel, sugar, olive oil and rosemary leaves, then pour this over the fish. Leave for eight hours before serving.

Savura of Fried Pilchards

1 kg sardines or anchovies
flour
oil for frying
salt and pepper

marinade:
¼ L olive oil
1/8 L red wine vinegar
2 sugarcubes
chopped parsley
4-5 cloves of garlic, chopped
rosemary
2 lemons
a few peppercorns
salt

Wash the fish, gut them and cut off their heads. Coat them well with flour and allow to rest for one to two hours. Then fry them in plenty of oil, arrange in a dish and season with salt and pepper. Grate the lemon peel, then squeeze out the juice. Boil these with the remaining ingredients for the marinade and pour over the fish.

Savura of Mackerel and Sardines

1 kg mackerel and sardines
flour
salt
oil for frying

marinade:
¼ L vinegar
¼ L olive oil
1/8 L water
2 bay leaves
a bit of rosemary
4 cloves of garlic, chopped
½ onion, sliced into thin rings
A few peppercorns

Clean, bone and filet the mackerel. Flour the filets and fry in hot oil, season with salt and arrange in a layer in a deep dish. Sardines may be left whole, but do clean them and remove the heads, then flour, fry and arrange on top of the mackerel.

Bring all of the ingredients for the marinade to a gentle boil for 10 to 15 minutes. Allow to cool, then pour over the fish and leave it for one or two days. Serve with cooked kale.

Savura of Grilled Fish

1 kg mackerel, sardines, tuna or bonito
¼ L of olive oil
1 large onion, chopped
1 carrot, julienned
1 stalk of celery, julienned
a bit of chopped parsley
4 cloves of garlic, chopped
a few peppercorns
a small handful of rosemary leaves
1 bay leaf
red wine vinegar
lemon

Whatever combination of rich, oily fish you will use, clean it well, cut the larger fish into steaks, then grill over wood embers until cooked. Arrange the fish in a plate or baking dish with raised sides.

Heat the olive oil and saute the onion, carrot, celery and parsley. When these begin to be tender, add the peppercorns, rosemary and bay leaf. Then add a few tablespoons of vinegar and pour over the cooked fish while still hot, making certain that all of the fish is coated. Cover and allow to marinate for at least eight hours. Thus prepared, the fish will remain tasty and succulent for several days. Serve chilled with lemon juice.

Savura of Octopus and Mussels

1 kg octopus
50 dag mussels in shell
1 large red pepper, small diced
1 large red onion, small diced
6 cloves of garlic, chopped
4 tbsp. chopped fennel
2 tbsp. chopped rosemary
a handful of capers
salt and pepper to taste
1 cup of olive oil
1 cup of red wine vinegar
juice of one lemon

Mix the onion, garlic, red pepper, herbs, capers and lemon juice in a mixing bowl. Add the olive oil and vinegar and blend vigorously with a whisk. Add salt and pepper to taste, then set aside.

Clean the mussels of their beards, and the octopus of its innards and beak. Cook the octopus in gently boiling water with a wine cork until tender. Remove from the water and allow to cool on a board. Cut the octopus into fork sized pieces and add to the marinade.

Steam the mussels until they are opened and cooked. You may simply boil them in the same water as the octopus was cooked, so long it has been skimmed of any debris. Remove the meat from the shells. Add these to the marinade, and stir everything well for full coverage. Season with salt and pepper to taste, then cover and refrigerate for at least eight hours. Serve as a cold side dish with a summer meal.

Octopus Salad

an octopus
1 large onion
A few cloves of garlic
1 dL wine vinegar
1 dL olive oil
salt and pepper
1 bunch of parsley leaves
1 lemon

Boil the octopus until tender, then rinse. Pull off the thin membrane of skin, then cut into bite sized pieces. Toss in a bowl with the olive oil, vinegar, salt, pepper, chopped parsley, onion and garlic. Allow to stand for at least an hour.

FRIED FISH

Fried River Eel

eel
salt
flour
oil for frying
lemon
parsley
breadcrumbs
white wine

Remove the heads and organs, then wash the eels and cut them into a long pieces. Season with a little salt. Mix flour, breadcrumbs and chopped parsley, then coat the eel pieces with this mixture. Allow to rest for a bit, then fry gently in plenty of oil over a medium flame. Drain on paper and sprinkle with a little white wine, then serve with lemon slices.

Fried Smelts

smelts
milk
flour
oil for frying
salt
lemon juice

Wash the fish, then soak for an hour in salted water or milk. Remove from the liquid and allow them to dry completely. Coat them with flour and fry in hot oil until they are a nice color. Sprinkle with lemon juice and serve with a green salad. The frying oil can be filtered and used in other dishes to add flavor.

Fried Squid

squid
flour
oil for frying
salt

Clean the squid thoroughly, being sure to remove the central bone. Wash and cut the bodies into rings, allow to dry slightly, then coat the rings and tentacles in flour and fry quickly in abundant oil. Sprinkle with salt and serve immediately with green salad. If the squid are large, boil them for a bit before flouring and fry in oil. Cuttlefish can be prepared in this same manner.

Fried Sardines

sardines
flour
oil for frying
lemon

Gut the sardines, remove the heads, rinse and pat dry. Coat them with flour and allow to rest for half an hour. Fry in hot oil and serve with lemon and green salad.

Fried Red Mullets

small red mullets
flour
salt
oil for frying

Remove the heads and organs and rinse well. Coat them with the flour, fry in hot oil and serve with green salad or cooked cauliflower.

Fried Hake

hake
flour
lemon
oil for frying

Remove the organs, rinse, coat with flour and fry in hot oil. Serve with lemon slices. For larger hake, remove the heads and cut into pieces before flouring and frying.

ROASTED FISH

River Eel the Dalmatian Way

eel
salt and pepper
parsley garlic
bay leaf
olive oil
lemon juice

Clean the eel and cut into pieces. Place in a roasting pan with a little pepper and salt. Sprinkle with chopped parsley and add a bay leaf to the pan. Pour olive oil and some lemon juice over the eel and roast in the oven. This method can also be used to prepare mackerel or sardines.

Stuffed Squid

24 medium or small squid
25 dag of homemade bread, cut into slices
25 dag grouper filet
4 salted anchovies
1 leek
1 clove of garlic
4 egg yolks
½ L milk
black olives
basil
parsley
olive oil

For the sauce:
3 dL tomato puree
1 onion
1 clove of garlic
1 bay leaf
dry white wine
olive oil

Soak bread in milk for ten minutes, then drain. Clean the squid tentacles and chop them. Finely chop the leek and parsley and fry in oil, add the squid tentacles, chopped olives, grouper and anchovies. Allow to cool and crush the grouper meat with fork. Pour the mixture into a bowl and mix well with the soaked bread, chopped basil and garlic, egg yolks, salt and pepper. Stuff the mixture into the cleaned squid bodies and secure them closed with toothpicks.

For the sauce, chop onion and garlic and oil. Add tomato puree, a glass of white wine and crushed bay leaf. Simmer for 5 minutes.

Pour the sauce into an ovenproof dish, arrange the squid on it and bake in a hot oven for 30 minutes, covering with aluminum foil after the first 15 minutes.

Stuffed Sardines

large sardines
grated hard cheese
garlic
parsley
bread crumbs
olive oil
red onion
salt and pepper

Cut open the bellies of the sardines from head to tail. Clean them of their innards, remove the heads and pull out the bones. If there are broken or partially disintegrated fish, clean and bone them, chop the meat finely and add it to the stuffing.

In a mixing bowl you will add grated hard cheese such as Parmigiano Reggiano or Grana Padano in an amount nearly equal to the weight of the fish. Add to this some finely chopped garlic and parsley, bread crumbs, salt and pepper. Blend in enough olive oil so that the mixture holds its shape when compressed slightly.

Roll each of the sardines around a spoonful of this mixture and arrange snugly in a baking dish. Pour over heated olive oil, and sprinkle with chopped parsley and thinly sliced onion. Bake in the oven for half an hour, adding a little wine to the bottom of the dish if it becomes too dry.

Roasted Bonito

1 kg bonito
lemon peel
6 cloves of garlic, chopped
a bit of chopped parsley
¼ L olive oil
1 cup red wine vinegar
salt and pepper

Clean the bonito, cut into steaks and arrange in a lightly oiled roasting pan. Sprinkle these with chopped lemon peel, garlic, parsley, salt and pepper, then pour over the remaining olive oil. Bake in medium high oven. Turn the fish over in the pan several times for even browning on all sizes. In the last five minutes of cooking, pour a glass of red wine vinegar over the steaks. Serve immediately with potato salad.

Octopus with Potatoes

1 large octopus
1 kg medium potatoes
3 large onions
6 cloves garlic, rough chopped
olive oil
1 cup wine (red or white)
¼ cup chopped Italian parsley
2 tbsp. chopped rosemary
coarse sea salt and cracked black pepper

Remove the beak and innards of the octopus and clean well. You may tenderize the octopus by pounding with a mallet or rolling pin if desired. Oil the bottom of a baking dish. Cut the onions into eighths and line the bottom of the pan with them. Season the onions with a few pinches of salt, pepper, garlic and herbs. Arrange the octopus on the onions so that it covers them as much as possible. Season as above. Cut the potatoes into wedges. Toss them in a bowl with olive oil, salt, pepper and herbs so that they are well coated. Cover the octopus with the potatoes. Pour wine over the assembly, drizzle with a bit more olive oil, then sprinkle the remaining garlic and herbs on top.

Cover the baking dish with its lid or aluminum foil, then roast in a very hot oven for 30 minutes. Pull the octopus from beneath the potatoes and place it on top of them. Cover and roast again for another 30-45 minutes, or until desired tenderness is achieved. Serve the octopus on the roasted potatoes and onions, and drizzle well with the juices. This dish is traditionally prepared in the peka with wood coals.

IX. MEAT, FOWL AND GAME

Mediterranean diets such as that in Dalmatia dictate that meat should not be eaten too often, and should be accompanied with plenty of vegetables and salads. Excessive meat intake produces a variety of toxins in the body that can spread and accumulate in the organs and joints, causing gout, kidney and gall stones, arteriosclerosis, diabetes and other unpleasantness. Meat does deliver high protein and vital nutrients, however. When eaten in moderation it can be a delicious and nutritious addition to the diet. Dalmatian cuisine features many sumptuous dishes made from meat, fowl and game.

BEEF

Beef Pot Roast with Garlic

1 kg chuck roast
3 tbsp. salt
4-5 cloves of garlic
10 peppercorns
tbsp. coriander
vegetables for soup
sauerkraut
a piece of dried meat or prosciutto

Chop the garlic, grind the spices and mix with the salt into a paste. Rub this over the entire roast, then place the roast in a big dish, load with a weighted board and allow to cure in the refrigerator for a couple of days. Wash well and simmer slowly in water until very tender with soup vegetables (carrot, celery root, parsley, etc.). Serve with sauerkraut that has been braised with some dried meat or prosciutto.

Round Roast with Celery

60 dag of beef from the leg
flour
2 tbsp. fat
1 onion
celery stalks
10 tomatoes
Salt and pepper

Cut the beef into pieces for stew and roll it in flour. Fry in fat with chopped onion, then add chopped celery. Add the starined juice of the tomatoes, salt and pepper and simmer for two hours, adding some broth or water as needed.

Brudet of Beef

65 dag beef cutlets
salt and pepper
4 onions
tomato
garlic
parsley
2 dL olive oil

Tenderize the cutlets with a mallet as if you would grill them, then put them in a pot with sliced onion and tomatoes, chopped garlic and parsley and pepper. Mix well in the pot with oil, cover and cook over a very low flame without water for 1½ - 2 hours until the beef is very tender. Season to taste with salt.

Beef with Lentils

60 dag beef
20 dag cooked lentils
salt and pepper
2 dag sliced bacon
2 onions
1 carrot
4 cloves of garlic

Cut the beef into pieces, season with salt and tenderize with a mallet. Lightly fry in heated oil the bacon, sliced carrots, chopped onion and garlic. Coat the beef with flour and fry with the other ingredients. Season with salt and pepper, add some water or broth and simmer for 2 hours. When the meat is tender, add cooked, drained lentils. Simmer together for a while.

Beef Goulash

60 dag juicy beef shoulder
60 dag potatoes
1 tbsp. fat
3-4 onions
broth or water
salt and pepper
a little marjoram
a little paprika

Heat the fat and fry chopped onions in it, then add the sliced meat and fry, stirring continuously until a sauce begins to build and thicken. Add some broth or water, season with salt and pepper to taste, add diced potatoes, some minced marjoram and paprika and cook for two and a half hours.

Braised Beef

50 dag beef sirloin cutlets
2 cloves garlic
5-6 cloves
1 tbsp. fat
1 onion
broth
3-4 tbsp. red wine vinegar
½ cup sherry
tomato juice

Beat the sirloin cutlets with a mallet. Heat the fat and fry the chopped onion, then add the meat and brown on all sides. Add some broth, cloves, sherry and simmer for a bit, then add the tomato juice and simmer on a low flame until very tender for about 3 hours.

Beef Stuffed with Rice

beef cutlets
salt and pepper
1 tbsp. fat
plenty of onions
3 tbsp. rice
nutmeg
flour
broth or water
1 tbsp. tomato paste

Season the cutlets with salt and pound thin with a mallet. Fry finely chopped onion in the fat, add rice, salt, pepper and a little grated nutmeg, and fry gently some more. On each piece of meat put a spoonful of the rice mixture, fold over and secure with toothpicks. Dust each cutlet with flour and brown on all sides in hot fat or oil. Add some broth mixed with tomato paste to the pan and simmer for one hour, shaking gently a few times. Remove the toothpicks before serving.

Beef Stuffed with Bacon and Garlic

60 dag beef sirloin cutlets
15 dag smoked bacon
5 cloves of garlic
parsley
salt and pepper
flour
fat or oil
broth or water
1 tbsp. tomato paste

Make a paste of minced bacon, garlic and parsley. Put a teaspoon of the mixture on each cutlet, then fold over and secure closed with toothpicks. Dust the cutlets with flour and brown on all sides, then add broth or water mixed with tomato paste and simmer on a very low flame for 2 hours. Serve with mashed potatoes.

Beef Tenderloin with Anchovy Butter

tenderloin steaks, sliced thick
olive oil
anchovy butter
chopped rosemary

Anchovy butter is prepared by mashing salt cured anchovy filets to a paste, then blending with butter. Oil the steaks and roast in a hot oven for approximately twenty minutes, brushing occasionally with softened anchovy butter. Sprinkle with chopped rosemary five minutes before steaks are finished cooking.

Dressed Beef Filet

1 beef tenderloin
5-6 potatoes
fat
salt
10 dag butter
2-3 eggs
a few tbsp. milk
prosciutto
breadcrumbs
smoked dry bacon

Flatten the filet with a mallet and fry on all sides in fat. Boil the potatoes, peel and mash with salt, hot milk, butter and egg yolks. Arrange the potato mixture on top of the filet, sprinkle with chopped prosciutto and breadcrumbs, then cover with slices of bacon. Roast the filet in a hot oven for about a half hour covered with aluminum foil.

Remove the foil and roast further until a nice color is achieved. Cut into slices, arrange on a plate and serve. This is a real treat!

Pržolica

beef rib roast
oil
powdered mustard
salt and pepper
5 tbsp. oil
flour

Cut the rib roast as boneless finger thick steaks, brush with oil, sprinkle with mustard powder and pepper, and place them in a baking dish under a weighted plate for a few hours to tenderize. Heat several hours between the two plates to soften. Flour the steaks on one side. Fry that side until a nice crust develops, season with salt, turn and fry the other side. Serve with chard and potatoes or green peas.

Pašticada

75 dag sirloin roast
a few cloves
4 cloves of garlic
smoked dry bacon
75 dag onions
10 dag of fat
1 celery root
salt and pepper
nutmeg
½ cup sherry or red wine
1 tbsp. tomato paste
2 cubes of sugar
broth or water

Wash the roast well, poke holes with a knife through it, then stuff the holes with pieces of sliced garlic and bacon. Poke the cloves into the meat. Put the meat into a dish and cover with wine vinegar, and allow to cure overnight.

Heat the fat in a deep saucepan and fry the meat on all sides until the juice runs out. Add the sherry or red wine in which you have dissolved the tomato paste, plus finely chopped onion and celery root, salt, pepper, sugar and grated nutmeg. Bring to a simmer, cover and cook on low heat for 3-4 hours, periodically adding water or broth to maintain enough cooking liquid. When the meat is tender, remove, cut into thick slices and arrange on a serving dish. Pass the juice and vegtables through a food mill to make a thick sauce, then return the meat slices to this sauce and simmer gently for a while. Serve with pasta or gnocchi. If the sauce is not thick and dark brown, you can fry some breadcrumbs and stir them in to thicken.

Pašticada of Trogir

75 dag beef roast
dry bacon
a few cloves
3 cloves of garlic
vinegar
flour
2 tbsp. fat or oil
1 onion
broth or water
1 tbsp. tomato paste
1/2 cup sherry or red wine
1-2 cubes of sugar
salt and pepper

Wash the roast well, poke holes with a knife through it, then stuff the holes with pieces of sliced garlic and bacon. Poke the cloves into the meat. Put the meat into a dish and cover with wine vinegar, and allow to cure overnight. Remove, drain well and coat well with flour.

Heat the fat or oil in a wide saucepan and brown the meat well on all sides, then add sliced onion, tomato paste, sugar, wine or sherry and water or broth to cover. Cover and simmer on a very low flame for 3 hours until tender remove the meat and slice. Pass the sauce through a food mill and return to the saucepan, season with salt and pepper, then add the meat slices and simmer on low heat for half an hour. You can add dried plums to the sauce at this time for a special touch. Serve with homemade pasta and sprinkle with grated cheese.

Meatless Pašticada

5 tbsp. oil
small onion
1 tbsp. flour
1 tbsp. tomato paste
½ cup sherry
12 dag dried plums
5-6 cloves
salt, pepper and nutmeg

In the hot oil fry chopped onion and stir in the flour. When well browned, add the tomato paste dissolved in cold water, sherry, chopped dried plums, cloves, salt, nutmeg and a little pepper. Simmer on a low flame for an hour and a half, adding water as needed so that the sauce does not become to thick. Serve with potato gnocchi and grated cheese.

Beef Tongue with Capers

beef tongue
smoked dry bacon
1 veal bone
3-4 carrots
parsley
1 turnip
celery and parsley root
1 bay leaf
1 large onion
3-4 cloves pepper
1 cup of rum or wine
2-3 handfuls of capers

In a pot place the tongue, chopped bacon, veal bone, a little parsley, sliced carrots, onion, turnip, parsley and celery root, bay leaf, cloves, pepper and rum or white wine. Cover with water or broth and cook for 3-4 hours on low heat. Peel the boiled tongue, cut into slices and arrange on a plate. Put the broth and vegetables through a food mill to make a thick sauce, season with salt and pepper, then heat again and add the cappers. Pour this sauce over the sliced tongue, and serve with mashed potatoes and peas.

Beef Tongue Samaštrani

beef tongue
salt
5-6 cloves of garlic
20 coriander seeds
vegetables for soup

Rub a mixture of salt, chopped garlic and crushed coriander seeds on the tongue so that it is well coated, put into a baking dish, cover with cellophane and a weighted plate or dish and allow to cure refrigerated for 3-4 days. Rinse it well and simmer in unsalted water with soup for 2-3 hours, until the skin peels easily from the tongue. Peel the tongue and slice it, and arrange on a plate. Serve warm with some of the sauce from cooking, or cold with horseradish, capers, olives or vinegared shallots.

Braised Beef Tongue

1 beef tongue
2 tbsp. fat
2 onions
broth or water
salt
a bit of tomato paste

Wash the tongue well and drain. Heat the fat in a deep pot and fry sliced onions in it, then add the tongue and fry well on all sides. Add a bit of broth or water so that it comes halfway to the top of the tongue, then add tomato paste and a little salt and stir them into the liquid. Cover the pot and cook over a low flame for at least 3 hours, until tender. Peel the tongue and slice. Serve with the cooking juice and mashed potatoes or pasta.

Fried Beef Tongue

beef tongue
flour
1 egg
a little milk
breadcrumbs
oil

Simmer the tongue in water until it is half cooked and the skin peels away. Peel it, cut into thin slices and dust with flour. Dip it in egg beaten with a little milk, then breadcrumbs so that it is well coated. Fry the slices in abundant oil until crispy. Serve with a caper sauce, salted anchovies, grated horseradish mixed with lemon juice and a little sugar, or some other piquant sauce.

Pašticada of Beef Tongue

beef tongue
smoked dry bacon
garlic
a few cloves
flour
fat or oil
2 onions
glass of wine or sherry
dried plums or apples

Peel the skin from a half-boiled tongue. Poke holes into the togue and stuff them with pieces of sliced bacon and garlic. Coat the tongue well on all sides. Heat oil or fat in the bottom of a pot and fry chopped onions, then fry the floured tongue on all sides and add wine or sherry. When it comes to the boil, add some of the liquid in which the tongue was cooked. Simmer until tender. In the last half hour of cooking, add diced apples or chopped dried plums to the sauce. When the sauce is thick and the tongue os tender, slice the tongue and arrange on gnocchi or pasta, then pour the sauce. You can sprinkle some grated cheese when serving.

Beef Tongue in Anchovy Sauce

beef tongue
5-6 salted anchovies
4 tbsp. oil
broth
2 lemons
pickles
black olives

Boil the beef tongue until tender, peel off the skin and cut it into finger thick slices. Mince the filets of anchovy very finely, add oil, broth, the juice of 1 lemon and whisk together well (you may run this through an electric food mill for a fine consistency). Put the sauce in a pan, arrange the sliced tongue on top, cover and simmer over a low flame for a bit. When the meat has taken up a bit of the sauce, arrange in bowl, then pour the sauce and garnish with lemon slices, chopped pickles and black olives.

Beef Tripe

beef tripe
50 dag potatoes
1 onion
salt
10 dag smoked bacon
6 cloves of garlic
parsley
broth
salt and pepper
tomato juice or paste

Scrub the tripe in hot water until they are completely white. Simmer with a sliced onion in hot water, and add some salt after it cooks for a while. It will be quite a while until the tripe is tender. Add water as needed. When the tripe is very tender, cut into long, wide strips. Make a paste from minced bacon, garlic cloves and parsley. Fry this for a bit, then add the tripe sauté for a few minutes. Add some broth, salt, pepper and tomato juice or paste to cover. Add very thinly sliced potatoes and simmer for a while until the potato is cooked and sauce becomes thick. At the end of cooking, add a little lemon juice, then serve with grated cheese.

Beef Tripe with Capers

1 kg beef tripe
1 dL oil
2 onions
salt and pepper
glass of wine
capers
vinegar

Cook the beef tripe in salted water and cut like noodles when tender. Fry chopped onions in oil, then add the tripe, salt, pepper, a glass of wine, a cup of chopped capers and a little vinegar to taste. Simmer for a bit until the sauce begins to reduce, then serve with boiled potatoes.

Beef Tripe with Tomatoes

1½ kg beef tripe
1 dL oil
3 onions
a few fresh tomatoes
1 tbsp. tomato paste
5 dag smoked bacon
5 cloves of garlic
parsley
salt and pepper
broth
grated cheese

Simmer the tripe until it is very tender, then cut into strips. Fry chopped onions in the oil, add chopped tomatoes and tomato paste. Make a paste of chopped bacon, garlic, salt, pepper and parsley, and add this to the pot. Simmer for a bit, then add a little broth and simmer again until the sauce thickens. Sprinkle with grated cheese when serving.

Stuffed Cabbage

50 dag ground beef
5 dag smoked pork or prosciutto
white cabbage
1 L water
cup red wine vinegar
2 onions
a little garlic and parsley
1 tbsp. fat
tomato juice

Cut the core from the center of the cabbage and pull apart the leaves. Boil a liter of water with a cup of vinegar, add the cabbage, cover and cook for 5-6 minutes until the cabbage is tender. Remove from the pot and drain.

Finely chop one of the onions and fry it, then mix with the ground beef, chopped pork or ham, garlic, parsley, salt and pepper. Place a spoonful of the mixture on each cabbage leaf and roll them up tightly. Chop the other onion and fry it in fat in a wide pan, add tomato juice and simmer for a bit, then place the stuffed cabbage in the sauce, cover and simmer over very low heat for an hour or so. Serve with the sauce.

Stuffed Cabbage of Sinj (Arambašići)

1 head of pickled cabbage
60 dag beef
20 dag fresh pork
15 dag smoked bacon
5-6 dag lard
1 small beef soup bone
smoked pork or mutton
prosciutto or smoked tongue
broth or water
2 large onions
6 cloves of garlic
lemon peel
salt and pepper
cinnamon powder
2-3 crushed cloves
½ nutmeg, grated
1 tbsp. of fat

Chop the beef, fresh pork and smoked bacon very finely by hand with a knife, because this produces a better flavor than grinding in a machine. Add chopped onion, garlic, spices, lemon peel, salt and pepper. Mix this all together very well. Cut the core from the cabbage and separate the leaves. Place a spoonful of the meat mixture on each leaf and roll them up tightly starting at the spot where it was connected to the core.

Melt the fat in the bottom of an earthenware baking dish and arrange the stuffed cabbage leaves in it. Add the soup bone, pieces of dried pork or mutton, and prosciutto or smoked tongue between the cabbage leaves. Pour enough broth to cover the cabbage, then cover with a lid or aluminum foil and roast in a slow oven for 4-5 hours. Shake the dish periodically to ensure that the cabbage leaves do not stick to the dish. Arambašići are always best when prepared the day before serving. When there are no pickled cabbage heads, they can be made instead with grape leaves softened in boiling water, and some shredded sauerkraut should be added to the meat mixture for a good sour flavor.

Stuffed Cabbage of Benkovac

1 kg sirloin
50 dag fresh pork
25 dag smoked dry bacon
beef soup bone
1 onion
3-4 cloves of garlic
½ nutmeg, grated
cinnamon powder
salt and pepper
5-6 crushed cloves
1-2 eggs
leaves of pickled cabbage
1 teaspoon of fat

Cut the meats into small pieces and place in a bowl. Add chopped onion, garlic, spices, eggs, salt and pepper, and mix well. Place a bit of the mixture in the cabbage leaves and roll them tightly. Put some melted fat in the bottom of an earthenware baking dish, line it with any extra cabbage leaves and arrange the stuffed cabbage leaves thereupon. Put the beef bone in the center, pour water or broth to cover and bake very slowly for about 5 hours.

VEAL

Veal is very tender and cooks quickly. It is usually fried or braised in a pan if it is not grilled, and it is recommended that any fat in the pan should be well heated before adding the meat.

Veal Primorska

80 dag veal
2 tbsp. fat
2 tbsp. bread crumbs
1 tbsp. flour
3 onions
parsley
salt and pepper
broth or water
nutmeg
grated hard cheese

Cut the veal into cubes and put into a pot to simmer over medium heat until the juice is nearly evaporated. In a separate pan heat the fat and fry the breadcrumbs, flour and finely chopped onions. When the onions take on a nice color, stir in chopped parsley, then pour this over the veal and mix well. Season with salt and pepper and simmer for half an hour. Add a little grated nutmeg and cheese and simmer for another 10 minutes.

Pan Braised Veal

¾ kg veal leg
salt
1 dL oil
3 dag bacon
1 onion
a little sweet paprika
2 dag flour
2 tsp. tomato paste
½ cup white wine

Cut the veal leg into steaks, season with a little salt, fry
quickly on both sides in oil, then set aside on a plate. Dice
the bacon and onion and fry in the same oil with paprika
and the flour. Add the wine and a little water mixed with
the tomato paste and stir well into the fried onion mixture.
Return the veal to the pan and simmer until tender and a
nice sauce develops. Serve with roasted potatoes and peas.

Veal with Tuna

1½ kg veal leg
2 carrots
parsley
celery root
10-12 salted anchovy filets
25 dag preserved tuna
1 handful of capers

Put the veal leg into a pot with sliced carrots and celery
root, anchovies, tuna, chopped parsley and a handful of
capers. Add enough water to cover the meat and simmer

until the veal is tender, adding a little water or broth as necessary. Once cooked, remove the veal and chill it in the refrigerator. Run the remaining sauce through a food mill and mix with a little mayonnaise. Slice the veal and serve cold with this sauce.

Veal Pržolica

60-80 dag veal rib roast
6 tbsp. oil
salt
½ onion
nutmeg
parsley
glass of wine
fatty broth

Cut the rib roast into steaks and tenderize slightly with a mallet. Season with salt and half the oil, leave under a weighted plate for an hour, then grill on both sides. In a skillet heat the remaining oil and fry thinly sliced onion with a little nutmeg and chopped parsley. Add the wine and some broth and stir together, then add the steaks to this and simmer for a while, until the meat is cooked and the sauce is a little thicker. Serve with roasted potatoes.

Grilled Veal Liver

veal liver
salt and pepper
oil
a little sugar
lemon
mustard powder

Cut liver into thick slices, sprinkle with pepper and coat with olive oil. Leave between 2 plates for an hour then grill. Once cooked, season the liver with salt and a little sugar to taste. Mix lemon juice with a little mustard powder for a nice piquant sauce.

Breaded Veal Liver

veal liver
flour
egg
crumbs
salt
sweetened lemon juice

Slice the liver into thin cutlets. Season with salt, dip in flour, then beaten egg and breadcrumbs. Fry in hot fat or oil and serve with sweetened lemon juice.

Sour Braised Veal Liver

50 dag veal liver
milk
8 tbsp. oil
3-4 young onions
salt and pepper
2 sugarcubes
2 tbsp. red wine vinegar

Soak the liver in milk for an hour. Heat the oil and fry sliced onions, then add sliced liver therein and fry on both sides. Add the sugar cubes and vinegar and simmer, then season with salt and pepper. Lamb's liver can be prepared in this same way. If you prepare kidneys with this method, add sage to the pan rather than sugar and vinegar.

Veal Liver Paté

25 dag veal liver
10 dag bacon
1 tbsp. fat or oil
3 boiled eggs
salt and pepper
1 lemon

Grind cooked liver and bacon in a food mill, then mix with the oil or fat. Mix in the chopped boiled eggs, salt, pepper and lemon juice and grind again. Serve as an appetizer with twice-baked toasts.

Veal Salamura

1 kg tender veal roast
salt and pepper
4 onions
½ lemon
1 sage leaf
1 bay leaf
a few juniper berries
1 bunch parsley
white wine
cup sweet red wine vinegar
12 dag salted anchovies
l tbsp. capers
plenty of olive oil

Rub the roast with salt on all sides and place in a bowl. Add sliced lemon and two of the onions, sage and bay leaf, juniper berries, peppercorns and chopped parsley. Pour in red wine vinegar and enough white wine, and marinate for at least 24 hours, turning the roast over every few hours.

Gently simmer the meat in the marinade mixed with an equal quantity of water for up to an hour. Once cooked, drain and cool. Finely chop the remaining onions, anchovies, 1 tbsp. parsley and capers and mix with enough olive oil to make a nice sauce. Pour the sauce over the meat and refrigerate until use. Serve cold, cutting thin slices and covering each with some of the sauce. This is especially delicious on hot days, and it will keep in the refrigerator for a week.

Veal Loin

veal loin
salt and pepper
sage leaf
a bit of rosemary
bacon grease
onion
a few cloves
carrot
a little garlic
broth
l tomato and some tomato paste

Trim the bone from the loin, leaving it whole. Season all sides with salt, pepper, chopped sage and rosemary. Heat some bacon grease in an ovenproof saucepan and sear the meat well on all sides. Turn off the flame and add to the pan an onion cut in quarters, thick slices of bacon, a few cloves, sliced garlic and carrots. Roast well in a hot oven, adding a little broth every once in a while. Turn the meat once during roasting for an even color. Add chopped tomato and a little tomato paste to the pan and mix well during the last few minutes of roasting. When cooked, carve the loin into slices and arrange on a plate. Press the sauce and vegetables through a food mill and serve in a dish with the meat.

Veal Brain with Eggs

veal brains
1 tbsp. fat
1 small onion
salt and pepper
2 eggs
parsley

Wash the brains, blanch in boiling water for a few minutes, then plunge into ice cold water. Slice apart and clean out any vessels, bone and blood. Fry some chopped onion in the fat, then add the sliced brains and a little salt and pepper. Stir well, then add beaten eggs. Cook as scrambled eggs, sprinkle with chopped parsley and serve.

MUTTON

Stewed Mutton

60 dag mutton from the neck or back
a few peppercorns
salt
marjoram leaves
two onions
2 cloves of garlic
vegetables for soup (carrot, parsley and celery root, etc.)
1 tbsp. fat
1 tbsp. flour

Wash the meat well and put into a pot, cover with water and add some peppercorns, salt, marjoram leaves, a sliced onion, peeled garlic and soup vegetables. Simmer covered for 2 hours. When the meat is tender and well cooked, remove from the broth and cut into thick slices.

In a separate pan fry the onions in the fat, then stir in the flour and mix into a roux. Stir in a little broth and mix well, bring to a boil, then add to the pot of broth and vegetables and stir well. Press the vegetables through a food mill and stir back into the broth to make a thick sauce. Pour the sauce over the mutton and serve with dumplings or mashed potatoes.

Cold Leg of Mutton

1 mutton leg
3-4 cloves of garlic
smoked dry bacon
lemon
salt and pepper
marjoram leaves
2 carrots
1 onion
a little celery

anchovy sauce:
1 cup olive oil
½ cup red wine vinegar
4-5 salted anchovies
2-3 cloves of garlic
parsley
pepper
a little lemon peel
olives and capers

Wash the mutton leg, remove the bone and slice once lengthwise so it unrolls and lies flat. Chop the garlic, bacon and marjoram and mix it with lemon juice, salt and pepper. Put this mixture into the center of the meat, roll and tie well with twine. Simmer for two hours in salted water with carrots, celery and onion. When cooked, remove from the broth and cool.

Mix finely chopped anchovies, garlic, lemon peel and parsley with olive oil and vinegar. Beat well to emulsion and pour over the sliced meat. Garnish with chopped olives and capers and serve cold.

Pašticada of Mutton

1 kg mutton leg
cloves
dry bacon
garlic
4 tbsp. fat or oil
3 fairly large onions
broth
3 tbsp. vinegar
salt and pepper
2 cubes of sugar to taste
tomato paste
½ cup red wine or sherry

Remove the skin and bone from the mutton leg, then make a cut so that it lies flat. Poke holes in the meat and stuff with sliced garlic and bacon, then spike with a few cloves. Fry sliced onions in the fat or oil in a pot, then brown the meat on all sides. Add broth, cover and simmer for a while. Add vinegar, sugar, salt and pepper to taste, cover and simmer again, pouring broth with tomato paste dissolved in it as needed. When the meat is well cooked and tender, carve into thick slices and place in another saucepan. Press the cooking liquid with onions through a food mill and add it to the meat, then add the red wine or sherry and cook another 15 minutes. Serve with mashed potatoes or macaroni.

Mutton Salamura

80 dag mature mutton roast
2 carrots
celery
parsley
2 bay leaves
a few peppercorns
salt
1 onion
1½ cups white wine
½ cup red wine vinegar
fat
1 tbsp. flour

Slice or grate the carrots, celery and onion and boil with
the parsley, bay leaf, peppercorns, salt, wine and vinegar
for a few minutes. Allow to cool, then pour over the
mutton roast and allow to marinate overnight.

The next day, strain the vegetables from the brine and fry
them in fat. Add the roast and fry on all sides, then add the
brine and simmer until tender. Slice the roast and arrange
on a plate. Press the juices and vegetables through a food
mill, then heat in the pan again. Make a roux of fat and
flour and stir this into the simmering sauce to thicken.
Season to taste if needed, then pour over the meat. Serve
with mashed potatoes.

Kaštradina

Kaštradina is salt-cured, smoked and dried mutton. It is a favorite dish, especially in winter. The best sheep are to be had in autumn, as they are mature and fat for the slaughter. When the meat is cleaned, cut into pieces and ready for salting, cut short, shallow gashes in it so that the salt penetrates more easily. Crush peppercorns to taste and mix with the salt, then coat the meat evenly with this mixture and leave it for 5-6 days. Every two days turn the meat. The bucket or barrel in which the meat is kept should be wooden and odorless, and well washed. Meat should also be kept from the flies by covering with cloth. When you remove it from the salt, wash it well, dry with a cloth and drain, then hang it in fragrant wood smoke.The meat will be dry in 2-3 weeks.

Kaštradina with Cabbage

60 dag of smoked dry mutton
1 kg fresh cabbage or kale
10 dag smoked bacon
6 cloves of garlic
half bunch of parsley
50 dag potatoes
1 tbsp. tomato paste

Wash the smoked mutton in hot water, then simmer in unsalted water in a deep pot for about 2 hours. Add roughly chopped cabbage or kale and simmer together a half hour longer. Add sliced bacon, garlic, chopped parsley, potatoes and tomato paste to the pot and simmer until all is tender.

Sheep Stomach with Cabbage

sheep stomach
baking soda
12 dag rice
2 onions
4 cloves of garlic
some raisins
some finely chopped cabbage
salt and pepper
a piece of celery root
a piece of smoked bacon or pig foot
1 kg rough chopped cabbage
few tomatoes or tomato paste
50 dag potatoes

Add some baking soda to very hot water and clean the stomach in it, scrubbing with a knife until bright and clean. Mix together rice, chopped cabbage, onion and garlic, raisins, salt and pepper, then stuff into the stomach and tie the ends. Do not fill so tightly that the rice has no room to expand. Put into a pot of cold water with a piece of celery root, a halved onion and a piece of bacon or pig foot. Cover and simmer on low heat, then add the kilogram of cabbage roughly chopped and tomatoes or tomato paste. Season with salt and pepper and cook for half an hour. Add sliced potatoes and cook for half an hour more. Serve all together.

LAMB

Lamb Stewed with Pršut

25 dag slab of prosciutto
50 dag lamb
½ onion
2 carrots
2 tomatoes
celery and parsley
noodles

Simmer prosciutto for an hour in 2-3 liters of water. Add 50 dag of mature lamb, sliced onion, carrots, celery, chopped tomatoes and parsley and simmer another hour. When the meat is cooked, strain the broth and cook homemade noodles in it. Serve the vegetables and meat on the noodles with a little bit of broth poured over.

Lamb Shanks

lamb shanks
roots for soup (carrots, celery and parsley root)
salt and pepper
garlic
olive oil
vinegar

Wash the lamb shanks with hot, then cold water. Bring to a boil in water with the roots, add salt and simmer until very tender. Chill the shanks and place in a bowl. Sprinkle with finely chopped garlic, salt and pepper, then pour over some oil and vinegar and allow to sit awhile before serving.

Sweet and Sour Lamb Offal

lamb liver, lungs and heart
4-5 tbsp oil
1 onion
3 tbsp. red wine vinegar
2 sugarcubes
salt and pepper

Wash the liver, lung and heart very well, remove any plumbing and cut into strips like noodles. Fry thinly sliced onion in the oil, then add the offal and some pepper and fry until cooked. Add salt only when the cooking is finished lest the offal becomes tough. Dissolve the sugar in vinegar and stir this into the pan. Serve with boiled potatoes.

Lamb with Green Beans

60 dag lamb
1 onion
1 dL oil
1 carrot
50 dag green beans
tomato juice
4 dag bacon
4 cloves of garlic
a bit of parsley
salt and pepper
piece of prosciutto

Fry finely chopped onion in oil, then add the lamb cut into small pieces with a piece of prosciutto and brown well. Add chopped carrots and a little water or broth. Cut the green beans each into 2 or 3 pieces and blanch separately in hot water, then add them to the lamb with some tomato juice. Make a paste of finely minced bacon, garlic and parsley and stir this into the pan. Pour enough water or broth to cover, season with salt and pepper and simmer until all is tender.

Lamb Paprikaš

60 dag lamb
fat
1 large onion
paprika powder (hot or sweet)
flour
handful of capers
tomato juice

Fry the chopped onion in plenty of fat, then add paprika powder to taste. Cut the lamb into small pieces and coat with flour, then add to the onions and paprika and fry all together carefully so as not to scorch the paprika. Add some water or broth and tomato juice and simmer until tender. At the end of cooking, you can add a handful of capers. Serve with roasted potatoes.

Lamb Stuffed in Spinach

60 dag large leaf spinach
¼ kg boneless lamb leg
10 dag smoked pork or prosciutto
small onion
1 egg
salt and pepper
celery and a little parsley
6 tbsp. oil
·2 tbsp. flour
meat or vegetable broth

Remove the bone from the lamb leg and cut it into small pieces, then grind with chopped smoked pork or prosciutto. Mix well with finely chopped onion, egg, salt, pepper, chopped parsley and celery. Put a teaspoon of the mixture in each of the spinach leaves and roll up tightly, securing with toothpicks if necessary. Fry the flour in oil to make a light roux, then stir in some broth and bring to a boil. Reduce the flame to low and place the stuffed spinach leaves in the sauce. Season with salt and pepper, cover and simmer on a very low flame for about an hour. Serve with a little bit of the sauce on top.

Lamb Lovački

lamb leg or shoulder roast
garlic
smoked bacon
6 tbsp. oil
3 tbsp. red wine vinegar
salt and pepper
rosemary sprig
nutmeg

Poke holes in the meat and stuff with sliced garlic and bacon. Put into a roasting pan with oil, 2 tbsp. vinegar, a rosemary sprig and a few peppercorns and roast in a hot oven. When roasted and tender, cut into slices. Simmer a little grated nutmeg, chopped garlic and parsley in 1 tbsp. vinegar with some juices from the meat, and pour this over the slices. Serve with roasted potatoes.

Lamb Tripe

lamb tripe
salt and pepper
2 tbsp. fat
1 onion
6 cloves of garlic
parsley
6 dag bacon
tomato juice
grated cheese

Rub the tripe well with salt between your hands and wash in warm water several times. Boil them in water and add a little salt, then simmer slowly for as long as it takes for them to be tender. Drain and cut into thin pieces. Make a paste from minced garlic, bacon and parsley and fry this with chopped onion. Add the tripe and fry for a bit, then add some water, tomato juice and pepper and stew until thick. Serve with roasted potatoes and sprinkle with cheese.

Vitalac

lamb intestines, heart, lungs, liver, spleen
salt and pepper
oil

This is a specialty of the isle of Brač that arrived with Greek settlers centuries ago. Wash the lamb intestines completely and dry them with a clean cloth. Cut the other organs into medium sized pieces and arrange them on a spit for fire roasting. Season them well with salt and pepper, then wrap the intestines around the organs several times so that they are completely covered. Roast over slow glowing wood coals for an hour, turning often to cook evenly. When cooked, remove from the spit and cut into pieces. Pour over some olive oil and pepper, and serve with green onions.

Šiša

lamb tripe
2 tbsp. fat
1 onion
2 carrots
salt and pepper
25 dag green beans
handful of peas
a potato
25 dag homemade noodles

Clean the trip well and boil until they begin to be tender, then, drain well and slice into thin strips like noodles. Fry chopped onion in the fat, add the tripe, sliced carrots and green beans, peas, diced potato and a little pepper. Add some water or broth and simmer gently until all is tender, then add noodles and simmer further until they are cooked.

Grilled Lamb's Liver and Heart

lamb liver and heart
olive oil
salt and pepper

Wash and drain the liver and the heart, cut them into equal slices, then season well in a bowl with oil, salt and pepper. Allow to rest for a while. Grill gently on slow coals taking care not to burn. When cooked, brush the meat with more oil, season with salt to taste and serve hot with fresh green onions.

Spit Roasted Whole Lamb

1 lamb
salt

Clean the lamb with a damp cloth, then rub with salt over every surface inside and out. Affix the lamb securely to a long stick, rest the ends of the stick on stones next to wood coals and roast, turning constantly. You can occasionally brush the lamb with a rosemary branch dipped in melted bacon grease, and even throw some rosemary onto the coals. The lamb will be cooked after 2-3 hours. Serve with a salad and green onions.

Stuffed Whole Lamb

whole lamb, lamb tripe, liver, lungs, heart, spleen, blood
salt
4 slices bread
white pepper
ground cinnamon, nutmeg and cloves
2 eggs
rosemary sprigs

Clean the lamb with a damp cloth. Clean all of the organs and remove the plumbing, put into a pot of cold water with the blood and bring to a boil, then add salt. When half cooked, remove the organs from the water and mince very finely, then mix well with chopped bread, white pepper, nutmeg, cinnamon, cloves and beaten eggs. Mix very well to an even consistency and form into a ball. Secure the lamb to the spit, sew the stuffing into the belly and roast near glowing wood coals, turning slowly all the while.

Brush the lumb with a rosemary branch dipped in hot bacon grease during cooking, and with salted water at the end. Cut the stuffing into slices and serve with the roasted lamb and green onions.

PORK

Pigs are usually slaughtered from mid-November to February, when the weather is cold and there are no insects to bring pathogens to the meat. When the pig is killed and bled, the carcass is quickly scrubbed with very hot water to clean it and ease the removal of hair. Take a very sharp knife in the opposite direction of hair growth. Once the hair has been removed, quickly hang the pig and make a long cut from neck to belly. Remove the stomach and intestines first, then gall bladder, liver, lungs, heart and kidneys. Wash all surfaces of the pig well again and hang in a cool, dry place until you are ready to divide the pig into cuts.

To prepare the intestines for sausage, empty them while still warm, then flush them out several times with plenty of fresh water. Once completely clean, salt them very thoroughly and store this way until you are ready to use them. Before filling, soak the intestine in warm water overnight with fragrant herbs tied in a piece of cloth. Good herbs to use are rosemary, marjoram, bay leaf and sage. After filling, sausages for long-term storage should be dried for one day, then smoked for at least 4-5 days.

The head can be cooked fresh, or smoked and dried for later use. It can be used for a variety of fresh and cooked sausages, or head cheese. The feet are usually smoked and used to flavor soups, stews and other dishes, or cooked into gelatin.

The heart, liver and kidneys are always prepared fresh in various ways, with the preferred method being simple grilling with salt, pepper and a little olive oil.

The best way to enjoy pork is to cook the whole pig at once on a spit over wood coals. Suckling pigs can thus be cooked at the age of 5-6 weeks.

Methods of preserving the meat can include a combination of curing in dry salt or wet brines, drying in the winter wind and smoking over a period of days, weeks or months. People living near the clean waters of the Adriatic can simply brine pork in sea water.

One delicious way to preserve the meat of an entire pig involves a spiced brine. For 100 kilograms of meat you will need:

60 L water
8 kg salt
½ kg sugar
5 cloves of garlic, crushed
5 cloves, crushed
a handful of peppercorns
a few bay leaves

Bring half of the water to a boil with all of the other ingredients, then add the rest of the water and stir well. Pour this over the meat in barrel. Turn the meat in the brine every three days. Smaller pieces of pork will be ready for cooking, or drying and smoking, in 1-2 weeks, whereas the hams require 5-6 weeks.

Dry curing in salt can be done in wooden barrels, and minced garlic and ground pepper can be rubbed over the meat to deter flies. Simply cover all of the butchered meat well with salt and place it in the barrel, then place a board on top and load it with stones. The weight aids the salt in penetrating the meat by pressing out moisture. Turn the meat every eight days and be certain that it remains coated. When the meat is cured after 2-4 weeks, wash and air dry well before hanging to smoke. Smaller cuts should be smoked for 2-3 weeks, larger ones for 5-6 weeks.

When curing the whole hams for pršut (prosciutto) rub them well with salt and a paste of crushed garlic and pepper. Place a few peppercorns in the fat end of the ham between the exposed thigh bone and the meat to help prevent spoilage. Put them in a barrel and load heavy stones on a clean board atop the hams to press out moisture. Apply more salt as needed every few days. When the meat is completely cured, wash and hang to dry in the air for two days, then hang to smoke and dry in cold air over winter. Hams can also be cured in a brine of pure seawater, then loaded with stones to press out the water before drying and smoking. The hams should dry and age in a clean, cool place such as a cellar or attic for about a year before slicing, and you may smoke them during this time as desired.

The bacon is best dry-cured in pure salt for 3-4 days with some weight loaded on top. Once cured, wash, cut it into smaller pieces, dry in the cool air for one day, then hang in smoke for at least a week and dry well in cold air.

To render lard, pour a little milk in the bottom of a pan and add a piece of onion. Add the fat and scraps cut into small pieces and simmer on low heat until all of the fat has been rendered and the scraps become crispy. Drain away the fat and cool it, then store in jars. The crispy scraps (*čvarci*) can be salted and eaten as a snack, or crushed and used in other dishes for flavor. Mixing crushed fat cracklings into bread dough is one delicious use.

Pork Ribs with Cabbage

60-80 dag fresh pork ribs
1 kg cabbage
3 tbsp. fat
5 dag smoked bacon
6 cloves of garlic
parsley
tomato paste

Boil chopped cabbage for a bit in salted water, then drain. Fry the ribs on both sides in fat, then add the cabbage, some tomato paste, and a paste of finely minced bacon, garlic and parsley. Mix well, add a little water or broth and simmer gently for 2 hours, stirring and adding liquid as needed.

Braised Smoked Pork

smoked dry pork
pickled cabbage, dry beans or barley

Wash the smoked meat well in warm water, then in cold. Cook slowly in unsalted water for up to two hours, depending on the age and dryness of the meat. This is usually cooked in winter with pickled cabbage, dry beans, barley and the like.

Pig's Head

pig's head
4-5 bay leaves
vegetables for soup
a few tbsp. vinegar
salt and pepper
1 large onion
oil and vinegar

Wash the pig's head very well in hot water, split it open and remove the brains. Boil in water with soup vegetables, add bay leaves, vinegar, salt and pepper. When the head is fully cooked, the meat will come away from the bones easily. Remove from the pot and drain, and pull the meat from the bones while still hot, then run through a meat grinder. Immediately wrap the meat in a clean cloth, tie into a ball and chill. When firm, cut the meat into thin slices and serve on bread with sliced onion, salt, pepper, oil and vinegar. This makes a fine lunch!

Pig's Feet

fresh or smoked pig's feet
vegetables for soup
oil and vinegar
pickled baby onions or shallots

Scrub the feet very well in hot water and be sure to remove any bristle with a sharp knife. Simmer gently for 3-4 hours in water with vegetables for soup. When tender remove from heat. Pour a little cold water in the broth and skim the fat from the surface. Strain the broth through a sieve into a serving bowl and serve the pig's feet in it. Eat with bread, pickled onions or shallots, and seasoned oil and vinegar. They are also delicious cooked in sauerkraut. You can simmer the bones further in the remaining broth to make gelatin.

Pork Kidney and Liver

2 pork kidneys
25 dag pork liver
6 tbsp. oil
2 onions
2 sage leaves
½ tbsp. flour
salt

Wash the kidneys well in cold water and remove the plumbing, then cut into thin slices. You can soak the slices in milk for an hour to help remove odor. Fry thinly sliced onions in oil, then add a little water. When the onions are browned and soft, add the kidney slices with two sage leaves and simmer, adding a little water if needed. Once tender, add sliced liver and simmer all together until tender. Sprinkle flour in the pan and stir, season with a little salt. Serve with mashed potatoes.

Pork Brisket Salamura

60 dag pork brisket
4 tbsp. fat
½ lemon
1 tbsp. flour

brine:
celery, parsley
2 carrots
1 onion
4 bay leaves
5-6 peppercorns
pinch of salt
cup red wine vinegar

Boil sliced celery, carrots and onions, chopped parsley, bay leaves, peppercorns, salt and vinegar in two liters of water, then cool. Add the pork brisket to the brine and leave overnight. The next day, heat fat in a wide saucepan, then add the meat and simmer gently until the juices have cooked out, then add a little of the brining liquid and simmer a while longer. When the meat is tender, slice and arrange on a plate. In a separate pan make a roux from the flour and some fat, then stir in strained lemon juice and some cooked juices from the pork. Pour this sauce over the meat and serve.

Pork Paprikaš with Sauerkraut

50 dag boneless pork cutlets
50 dag shredded sauerkraut
1 tbsp. fat
1 large red onion
1 red pepper
paprika powder
smoked bacon
garlic
parsley
1 tbsp. tomato paste

Fry finely chopped onion in the fat, then add sliced red pepper and a little paprika powder. Stir together, add the pork cutlets and simmer, stirring and adding a little broth or water as needed. Add the sauerkraut and simmer, stirring often. When all is tender and well cooked, stir in a paste of finely minced bacon, garlic and parsley, and the tomato paste.

Baked Pršut

1 whole prosciutto ham
wheat flour
water

Wash the ham well. Make an elastic dough from flour and water and wrap this completely around the ham. Bake for 2-3 hourts, depending on the size of the ham. Leave in the crust for day, then remove the crust, slice the ham and serve.

Stewed Pršut

1 whole prosciutto ham
water or red wine

Wash the ham well in warm water, then cover completely with water and simmer for several hours until tender. This is even better if you use red wine instead of water. Cut it when cool and serve with sour salad.

Fresh Ham Baked in Pastry

1 fresh pork leg
salt
1 head of garlic
wheat flour
water

Coat the pork leg well with plenty of salt that has been mixed with crushed garlic and leave for 3-4 days with a weighted board on top. Make a dough of flour and water and roll it out thinly. Wrap the pork leg in the dough and bake in a roasting dish in a medium oven. When the dough gets a nice crust, add a little hot water to the dish and bake for about 2 hours more. Allow the ham to cool in the dough. Slice the ham thinly and serve with pickles or a sour salad.

Roasted Pork Loin

60 dag pork loin
salt
smoked bacon
lemon
pork caul fat
5 tbsp. oil
5 cloves of garlic
parsley

Season the pork loin with salt and lay thinly sliced bacon and lemon slices on top. Wrap the caul fat around the loin, put it into a dish and roast in the oven, pouring a little water in the pan as needed. When just cooked, carve into thick slices and arrange in the baking dish. Mix the oil with finely chopped garlic, parsley and some of the pork juices in a bowl. Pour this over the meat and bake another half hour. Sprinkle lemon juice and serve.

Milk Roasted Pork

80 dag pork loin
3 dL milk
bread
water

Season the pork loin with salt, tie with twine and put into a baking dish with the milk. Cover and cook slowly until meat is tender and the milk has cooked out. Turn up the heat to brown the meat, then add a little water. Fry the sliced bread and serve the sliced pork on it with the pan juices.

Pork with Capers

½ kg pork steaks
salt
1 large onion
1 tbsp. capers
1 lemon
fat

Pound the steaks thin with a mallet and season with salt. Finely chop the onion and fry it lightly in fat, then add the meat and fry on both sides. Add chopped capers, cover and simmer until tender. Arrange the steaks on a plate, then add the juice of a lemon to the pan and stir. Pour the sauce over the steaks. Serve with fried potatoes.

Smoked Suckling Pig

1 small suckling pig
brine of salt, sugar, pepper and spices
cornflour
grated horseradish

Boil plenty of brine of water, salt, sugar, pepper and spices and allow to cool. Hold the suckling pig in this brine for a few days. Remove the pig from the brine, rinse well, then dust him all over with corn flour. Smoke the pig for 3-4 days. When well smoked and dried, wash in warm water and simmer gently in water in a deep pot until tender. Cut into slices and arrange on a plate in its original shape. Garnish with grated horseradish and serve hot.

Baked Suckling Pig

1 small suckling pig
salt
lemon
bacon grease
fat
beer

The best pig is 5-6 weeks old, since he is still sucking milk and his meat is particularly tasty. As soon as the pig is cleaned of its organs, cover inside and out with salt and allow to sit for an hour. Grease a roasting pan large enough with fat, lay a few sticks crosswise in it, then arrange the pig belly down on them. Coat the pig with lemon juice and bake in a medium oven. Baste often with the juices that run off during baking, plus lard or bacon grease and beer. Cook for 3 hours. When baked, make a cut in the neck to let out accumulated steam, then cut into pieces and arrange them on a plate in the pig's origianl shape. Serve with a green salad or sour vegetable salad..

Spit Roasted Suckling Pig

1 suckling pig
salt
bacon grease
rosemary sprig
lemon juice

Season the pig inside and out with salt and secure to a spit. Let it rest salted on the spit for 3 hours, then roast next to a hot wood fire, turning constantly for approximately 3 hours. Take care in maintaining the fire so that it does not get too hot and burn the pig. Baste frequently with a sprig of rosemary dipped in warm bacon fat. Serve warm with a green sald, or serve cold with lemon juice.

SAUSAGES AND CHARCUTERIE

Krvavica (Blood Sausage)

2 L pork blood
50 dag rice
a bit of roasted pork belly and rib meat
cinnamon
grated fresh lemon peel
ground nutmeg
parsley and onion
intestines for sausage

Cook the rice in boiling water for ten minutes, then drain and cool. Finely grind the roasted pork meat, mix it with finely chopped parsley and onion that you have fried a little in fat. Then mix in the lemon peel, ground spices, cooked rice and blood. Stir well, then fill the intestines with the mixture, taking care not to fill too tightly. Tie into links, simmer for half an hour in water, then allow them to cool. Grill the sausages and serve hot.

Kaštelanska Krvavica

intestines for sausage
60 dag rice
1 head of white cabbage
salt and pepper
handful of raisins
nutmeg
lemon peel
parsley
red onion
½ L water or broth

Finely chop the cabbage, add some salt, pepper, raisins, nutmeg, chopped onion, lemon peel and uncooked rice, Mix well, then add the water or broth. Fill the intestines with the mixture taking care not to fill too tightly so that the rice has room to expand while cooking. Tie into links and simmer in salted water for about an hour. Prick the sausages with a pin to allow air to escape while cooking. Allow them to cool and dry. You can even smoke them if desired. Grill or roast and serve hot.

Primorska Krvavica

3.5 L swine blood
60 dag corn flour
a bit of milk as needed
1 onion
parsley and cinnamon
salt and pepper
1 tbsp. crushed pork cracklings
a handful of raisins
a handful of dry corn kernels
cleaned pork intestines
some oil

Collect the blood of one pig in a bowl (approximately 3.5 liters) and stir to prevent clotting. Oil the bottom of another bowl, pour in a half liter or so of warm salted water, then sift in the corn flour and strain in the pork blood through a sieve. Stir all of this smooth, adding a bit of milk if the mixture becomes too thick. Finely chop the onion and fry it in a little fat, adding a bit of chopped parsley, ground cinnamon, raisins, crushed pork cracklings, salt and pepper. Add this to the blood and corn mixture and mix well. You can fry a spoonful of the mixture in a pan to check the seasoning and adjust for your taste.

Gently fill the intestines with the mixture, taking care not to fill too tightly. Tie the ends, and gently twist the filled intestine into links (you may use small knots of butcher's twine to secure the joint between individual links if you desire). Wash in cold water. Put a layer of dried corn kernels in the bottom of a deep pot, lay the links on top of this and cover with salted water (the corn kernels prevent the links from sticking to the bottom of the pot). Bring to a gentle simmer and cook 45 minutes to an hour. While they are cooking, prick the links with a pin to allow air to escape and prevent bursting.

When the krvavica is cooked and set, turn off the flame. Do not remove from the water until it has cooled completely. Lay them out on a board to drain. When they are dry, hang them in the smokehouse with cool smoke for a few days. Krvavica is best grilled or roasted, and served with sauerkraut.

Luganige

50 dag lean pork
25 dag bacon
salt
crushed peppercorns
crushed coriander seed
sheep's small intestine

Cut the bacon and trimmed pork into cubes and grind coarsely. Mix with salt, peppercorns and some coriander, knead with the hands very well and allow to rest overnight in the refrigerator. Stuff the mixture into intestines and tie into links, two together at a time. These can be smoked for a day or two if desired. Fry them a bit before cooking in soup with rice, or slice them and fry in fat before adding some pasta.

Garlic Pepper Sausages

3 kg pork belly meat
9 dag salt
½ dag ground pepper
1/8 L water
6-7 cloves of garlic
medium pork intestines

Dice the meat very finely with a knife. Add the salt, pepper, water and finely chopped garlic. Mix well with the hands for 15-20 minutes, then fill the intestines with the mixture and tie into links. Hang them in smoke for a few days, or even longer if you want to keep them for a long time. Grill over wood coals and serve.

Sinjska Kobasica

50 dag pork
15-20 dag beef
½ an onion
salt and pepper
½ lemon's peel
4-5 crushed cloves
ground nutmeg
4 cloves of garlic
a little fresh bacon
pig intestine

Mince the pork and beef very finely, add chopped onion and lemion peel, pepper, nutmeg, cloves, and garlic that has been crushed with salt. If the pork is not so fatty, add some chopped bacon to the mixture. Fill the intestines with the mixture, tie into links and hang in smoke for 8 days.

Salama

3 ½ kg beef shoulder roast
3 ½ kg pork leg
2 kg fresh bacon
10 dag salt
15 dag pepper
¾ L white wine
garlic
some oil
large beef intestines

Grind all the meats coarsely and knead in a bowl for 15 minutes with salt, pepper and white wine. Allow this mixtrue to rest and cure overnight, then stuff it into the beef intestine, tie and cut into links of 40-50 centimeters. Poke the links with a pin and press out any air. Tie a loop of twine on the end of each link and hang in spruce smoke for 2-3 days. Make a paste of crushed garlic, salt and a little oil and rub this over the links, then coat them in sifted ash. Hang in a cool, dark, dry place to dry. This can take several months, but you will appreciate the results.

Sinjska Salama

5 kg pork leg
2 kg juicy beef
2 kg fresh bacon
20 dag salt
6 dag crushed pepper
1/2 liters of water or broth
beef intestines

Finely chop the pork and beef, mix together well, then wrap tightly in a clean towel and hang it on a peg to drain for 24 hours. Put it into a bowl and mix with chopped bacon, salt and pepper, then mix together well. If the mixture is too thick, mix in a little water or broth. Fill the beef intestines with the mixture and tie into links. Allow to dry overnight, then hang in cool smoke for 8 days. Store in a cool, airy place to dry, and they will last all year. Cook with sauerkraut or stuffed cabbage leaves, or grill and serve with lemon juice.

Sinjski Sudžuk

5 kg fresh pork shoulder or leg
2 kg fresh bacon
15 dag salt
5 dag peppercorns
glass of water or broth
beef intestines
lemon

Finely chop the pork and beef, mix together well, then wrap tightly in a clean towel and hang it on a peg to drain for 24 hours. Mix in a bowl with cubed bacon, salt, cracked peppercorns and a little water or broth. Knead with the hands for 20 minutes, then fill the intestines with the mixture and hang to dry overnight. Put a weighted board on the sausages on the second day to flatten them a little and dry for one more day, than hang in cool smoke for 5 days. These can be cooked with sauerkraut or stuffed cabbage leaves, or grilled and served with lemon juice. You can also dry them completely for a long period and slice thinly as salami.

Stuffed Stomach

pig stomach
pig head
a couple of pig's feet
heart, tongue and kidneys
salt and pepper
clove and cinnamon powder
a few tbsp. vinegar

Wash the stomach well as described for preparing intestines. Boil the head, feet, heart, tongue and kidneys in water until all is tender, then drain, remove meat from bones and chop into thin strips. Add salt and pepper, cinnamon and cloves to taste. Mix in some of the cooking liquid with a little vinegar, then stuff the mixture into the stomach and sew it closed with twine. Cook the stomach in the broth, then drain and place a weighted board on top while it cools. You can slice and serve warm, or hang it in smoke to dry for long storage.

Hladetina

4 pig's feet
a few pieces of pig skin
pig head
3 tbsp. vinegar
salt
handful of parsley leaf
1 celery root
1 carrot
½ onion
2 cloves of garlic
10 peppercorns
2 bay leaves
2-3 tbsp. water
lemon
a couple of boiled eggs
salami
2 egg whites

Put the head, feet and skin in a pot and cover with salted water and a few tablespoons of vinegar. Simmer for an hour, then add sliced onion, carrot and celery root, parsley leaves, chopped garlic, peppercorns and bay leaves and simmer until all becomes tender and the broth is strong. Add a few tablespoons of cold water and allow the broth to cool and clarify for an hour or so. Skim and discard the fat on the surface. Remove all of the meat from the bones and chop coarsely, then mix with some diced salami. Put this into a porcelain dish leaving a finger width of space on top, and lay lemon and boiled egg slices on top.

Clarify the broth by simmering with egg whites for 45 minutes, then strain it through a clean cloth. Gently pour the broth over the meat in the dish to a finger width above the meat, then chill in the refrigerator until the broth is jelly. When solid, remove from the dish. Serve cold slices with chopped onion, oil and vinegar

Kranjska Kobasica

6 kg fresh pork shoulder
18 dag salt
1 dag cracked pepper
1/4 L water
1 head of garlic
pig intestine

Finely mince or grind the pork and mix with salt and cracked pepper. Crush the garlic well and simmer in a little water for a few minutes, then add this to the meat mixture. Mix well, then stuff into the intestines and tie into links. Hang them to dry overnight, then hang in dry smoke for 3 days. Once smoked and dried, these can be stored in a deep container covered in rendered fat so that the air cannot get to them. Keep the container in a cool, dark place until use. To cook, simmer them in water for up to an hour. Serve hot with sauerkraut, horseradish and mustard.

FOWL

With regard to flavor and juiciness, every bird has its own season. Old hens and young capons are best in winter. Chickens are best in late spring and summer. Domesticated ducks are best when fattened up in winter, and turkeys are good from October until March.

When the bird has been killed, pour warm water over the body to loosen the feathers. Hold the bird with one hand and pluck the feathers with the other. The feathers can be washed, dried and kept for pillows. Once plucked of the feathers, light a rolled piece of paper on fire and wave it slowly under the carcass to burn off any hairs or tiny feathers that remain.

Remove the head, then make a slit in the body at the base of the neck and at the hind end between the legs. Remove the organs carefully so that they do not rupture and taint the meat. Put the liver and gizzards in cold water to remove bitterness before cooking.

When cooking a large chicken in soup, cut in half lengthwise, then cut each half into three even pieces. If it is smaller, cut it into four pieces.

Cold Cock

1 rooster
8 tbsp. oil
1 large onion
1 tbsp. chopped parsley
3 salted anchovies
½ cup capers
a few tbsp. vinegar
1 lemon

Boil a whole rooster in water until completely cooked, then chill. Cut into pieces and arrange in a bowl. Mix together the oil, vinegar, chopped anchovies, onion, capers and parsley, then bring to a quick boil in a pan for 5 minutes. Add the juice of a lemon, stir well and remove from the heat. Pour this sauce over the meat, covering evenly. This is best when prepared in the morning and served in the evening.

Cock Under the Bell

1 rooster
salt
25 dag smoked bacon
1 tbsp. fat
1 dL olive oil
1 onion
3 carrots
1 pepper
1 kg potatoes

Clean the bird well, cut into large pieces and season with salt. Put them into the oiled roasting plate with thinly sliced bacon, halved potatoes, whole carrots and sliced pepper. Put a little fat on each piece of the bird. Cover the dish with the heated baking dome, bury in glowing coals and roast for an hour and a half.

Chicken with Parmesan Sauce

2 meaty young hens
vegetables for soup
salt
4 dag fat or butter
2 dag flour
6 egg yolks
cup grated Parmesan cheese
cup of grated horseradish
15 dag rice
fat
1 onion
butter

Clean the hens and cook them in salted water with soup vegetables until just cooked. Cool and pull all of the meat from the bones.

Make a roux from the flour and fat or butter, then stir in a few cups of the strained cooking liquid and bring to a boil. Mix the egg yolks and grated cheese in a bowl and gradually pour the heated sauce into it while whisking. Put the sauce back into the skillet, add the meat and stir so that it is covered with the sauce.

Fry the chopped onion in some fat, then stir in the rice and toast it a bit. Add enough water and simmer the rice until tender. Season with a little salt and stir in some butter. Put the rice onto a serving plate, then put the warm chicken meat with sauce on top and serve.

Chicken with Celery

1 pair of young chickens
salt
6 tbsp. fat
4 celery stalks

Cut the chickens into pieces, season with salt and fry on all sides in the fat. Remove from the pan and place on a plate. Slice the celery and add it to the pan juices, then return the chicken to the pan, cover and simmer for 20 minutes. Serve with roasted potatoes.

Pigeon with Bacon

pigeons
salt
smoked dry bacon
fat

Wash the pigeons well, season with salt and lay them in a roasting dish rubbed with fat. Put sliced bacon over the pigeons and roast them, basting continuously with the bacon drippings and juices. Serve with baked potatoes or steamed peas.

Duck with Celery Root

1 duck
4 tbsp. fat
2 large onions
4 celery roots
50 dag tomatoes
¼ L white wine or sherry
salt and white pepper

Rub 3 tablespoons of fat on the duck and roast in a hot oven. When it takes on a nice color, remove from the oven. Slice the onions and chop the celery root, fry them in a pot in the remaining fat, then add the whole duck to the pot with chopped tomatoes and wine or sherry. Season with salt and white pepper, cover and simmer until the duck is tender. Cut the duck into pieces and serve with the celery root and mashed potatoes.

Roast Duck

1 duck
1 apple
4 tbsp. fat
Salt

Season the duck with salt, put an apple inside it and place in a roasting pan rubbed with fat. Roast for about 2 hours, basting the duck with the juices every once in a while. Cut the duck into pieces and serve with salad.

Roast Goose

young goose
1 red onion
salt and pepper
4 cloves of garlic
parsley
3 eggs
1 large slice of bread
milk
4-5 tbsp. of fat

Clean the goose well, remove the wings and legs, then remove all of the meat with a knife, keeping the skeleton intact. Grind the meat coarsely. Fry chopped onion, garlic and parsley in fat. Soak the slice of bread in milk, then mix well in a bowl with the fried onion mixture, eggs and ground goose meat. Arrange this meat mixture on the skeleton of the goose, brush with a little melted fat and roast in the oven.

WILD GAME

Rabbits are the most popular wild game, and they are plentiful in the karst landscape of Dalmatia. Younger rabbits are better as their meat is more tender. Once killed, the rabbit should be gutted, but the skin should be left intact. Hang it in a cool, dry place to age for a couple of days. This allows the production of lactic acid in the meat, helping it to break down and become tender. Skin the rabbit and soak overnight in a brine with vinegar to tenderize it further. Wild ducks, geese, partridges, pheasants and snipe are also quite good. Once the feathers have been removed, hang them to age as with the rabbit. Rabbit is good from August to January. Partridge, quail and snipe are good from August to December, and wild ducks from July to February. Pigeons are best in summer and autumn, pheasant from mid-August to February.

Venison meat is very lean and therefore easy to digest. It is also best when the meat is brined overnight, roasted with oil or fat, and served with a strong, dark sauce.

Mallard with Sauerkraut

1 mallard
1 onion
15 dag smoked bacon
1 kg sauerkraut
broth
a few smoked sausages

Clean the duck and cut into pieces. Fry finely chopped onion and bacon in some fat, then arrange the duck pieces on top. Cover with the chopped sauerkraut and simmer for 20 minutes. Add a little vegetable or chicken broth, cover and stew for 2 hours on a low flame. Shake the pan every once in a while, but do not stir. Halfway through the cooking add sliced sausages. Serve with roasted potatoes.

Mallard with Lentils

1 mallard
25 dag lentils
4 tbsp. oil
salt and pepper
2 tbsp. fat
1 onion
4 cloves of garlic
1 carrot
parsley
3 celery stalks
1 glass of wine

Rub the mallard with oil, season with salt and roast in a hot oven just until it takes on a nice color. Boil the lentils until tender, drain and set aside. Fry chopped onion, carrot, celery and garlic in fat, add a little water and simmer until tender. Cut the mallard into pieces and arrange it in the pan with the vegetables. Add the juices from the mallard, a glass of wine, salt and pepper and simmer for half an hour. Add the lentils and simmer for another 15 minutes.

Braised Partridge

a partridge
oil
bacon
10 dag carrots
a few pieces of prosciutto
1 pickled cucumber
l tbsp. tomato paste
½ cup white wine
1 onion
2 potatoes
1 head of cabbage

Rub the partridge with oil inside and out and roast in a hot oven. Boil the cabbage in salted water. Fry diced bacon in a little oil, add sliced carrot, onion, chopped prosciutto and pickle, tomato paste and white wine. Stir well. Cut the partridge into pieces and add to the simmering vegetables with sliced potatoes. Cover with the boiled cabbage and a little water or broth and simmer over a low flame until all is very tender.

Rabbit the Dalmatian Way

1 rabbit
vinegar or sea water (brine)
garlic
smoked dry bacon
salt
2 cups oil
1 cup red wine vinegar
1 sage leaf
2-3 bay leaves
1 sprig of rosemary
white pepper
1 onion
1 carrot
2-3 lemons
1 cup sherry or wine
parsley

Brine the skinned rabbit overnight in sea water or diluted vinegar. Wash well, then poke holes in the meat and fill them with slices of garlic and bacon. If you brined the rabbit in vinegar, season it lightly with salt. Put into a roasting pan with a cup of oil, or two cups of oil if the rabbit is larger. Add the sage and bay leaves, rosemary sprig, sliced onion and carrot and roast in a low oven for about an hour, pouring over a little red wine vinegar a few times during the cooking. Cut the rabbit into pieces and arrange carefully in a skillet. Press the vegetables and juices through a food mill. Whisk together the juice from the lemons, a little oil and finely chopped garlic. Pour this over the rabbit with the pureed vegetables and juices. Bring to a rapid boil, then lower the heat, cover and simmer for another hour, adding a little sherry or wine and plenty of chopped parsley halfway through the cooking time. In some regions a few teaspoons of sugar are added to the sauce. Serve hot with dumplings or mashed potatoes, or serve cold sprinkled with lemon juice.

Rabbit the Sinj Way

rabbit
bacon
garlic
salt and peppercorns
plenty of rosemary
2 cups oil
½ cup red wine vinegar
½ cup red wine
3-4 sugarcubes

Poke holes in the rabbit and stuff them with sliced bacon and garlic. Season with salt and place in a pan with one cup of oil, vinegar a few peppercorns and chopped rosemary. Roast in the oven for an hour. Cut the rabbit in pieces and place back in the pan, then pour over another cup of oil, wine and the cooking juices. Add the sugar cubes, and simmer over a low heat until the juices thicken.

Roast Quail

a few quail
smoked bacon
4 tbsp. oil
1 lemon
salt and pepper

Put the quail in an oiled roasting dish and lay slices of bacon over them. Roast in the oven or under the peka. Pour the juices over them when serving, season with salt an pepper and a little lemon juice.

Woodcock with Toast

woodcock
smoked bacon
salt and pepper

For the toasts:
slices of white bread
woodcock liver
chicken liver
1 tbsp. finely chopped onion
1 egg
parsley
2-3 crushed juniper berries

Season the bird with salt and pepper and place breast down in an oiled roasting pan. Lay slices of bacon across the back and roast in the oven. Once cooked, drain the fat into a skillet and fry slices of bread in it. Mince the woodcock and chicken livers finely and mix with chopped onion, parsley, egg, salt, pepper and finely crushed juniper berries. Spread the mixture on the toasts and bake in a hot oven for five minutes, or until the liver is cooked. Serve with the roasted woodcock.

Roast Pheasant

1 pheasant
salt and pepper
5 tbsp. oil
1 tbsp. parsley
smoked bacon
some wine
½ lemon

Coat the pheasant with oil, season with salt and pepper and leave it for an hour. Wrap the pheasant in sliced bacon and secure the slices with toothpicks. Fry the bird on all sides in oil so that the bacon takes on a nice color, then roast in the oven until tender and all of the juices run clear. Periodically add a little water to the pan as needed. Cut the pheasant into pieces, pour over the pan juices and a little lemon juice. This is also delicious served cold with a little mayonnaise.

Venison

venison roast
brine
smoked bacon
2-3 tbsp. oil
a few sprigs of sage
a few sprigs of rosemary
salt and pepper
1 cup white wine
1 lemon
caper sauce (see Sauces and Condiments)

Brine the venison overnight, then rinse and pat dry with a clean cloth. Slice the bacon and fry it in oil, then add the venison, sprigs of sage and rosemary, white wine, salt and pepper. Cover and simmer gently. When the meat is tender, stir in strained lemon juice and caper sauce and simmer for another 15 minutes. Slice the meat and pour the sauce over it. Serve with roasted potatoes or gnocchi.

X. SAUCES AND CONDIMENTS

Sauces in Dalmatia are generally not as thick as those in other European cuisines. The recipes here include warm and cold sauces for cooked meats, fish, vegetables, pasta, dumplings and the like. Warm sauces often begin with a roux of flour toasted in heated fat, such as oil or rendered lard. Broth, cooking juices and other ingredients are added to the roux, and the sauce can be finished with a knob of butter for extra richness.

WARM SAUCES

Caper Sauce

3 tbsp. oil
1 tbsp. flour
broth or water
3 dag capers
a little lemon peel

Stir the flour into heated oil to make a roux. Add capers
and a little grated lemon peel and mix well. Stir in a little
water or broth, bring to a boil, then reduce heat and
simmer to thicken. Season with salt and pepper if desired.
Serve over roasted meats and fish.

Anchovy Caper Sauce

2 dL olive oil
3 salted anchovies
parsley
2 cloves of garlic
3 tbsp. capers
1-2 lemons
a little vinegar

Mince the anchovies to a fine paste and stir into heated oil.
Add chopped parsley, garlic and capers with the juice of
the lemons and vinegar. Bring to a boil, then allow to cool
before serving on hot meats.

Anchovy Sauce

3 tbsp. oil
1 tbsp. flour
3 salted anchovies
parsley
bread crumbs

Fry the flour in oil gently until it takes on a nice golden color. Add chopped anchovies, parsley, breadcrumbs and a little water or broth. Bring to a boil, then remove from heat and whisk well to an even consistency. Serve with meat.

Olive Sauce

1 tbsp. oil
1 tbsp. flour
2 tbsp. black olives
2 tbsp. capers
3 salted anchovies
pepper

Fry the flour in oil gently until it takes on a nice golden color, then add the pan juices from roasted fowl or some chicken broth, chopped olives, anchovies, capers and pepper. Bring to a boil, then reduce heat and simmer to thicken. Serve with poultry.

Garlic Sauce

1 tsp. garlic
1 tsp. parsley
broth or water
salt

Make a light roux from flour and oil and add crushed garlic and chopped parsley. Add some broth or water, season with salt and serve on roast meat, poultry or fish.

Šalša (Tomato Sauce)

1 kg tomatoes
1 bunch parsley
8 cloves of garlic
1 dL olive oil
salt and pepper
basil leaves

Mix oil, crushed tomatoes, chopped parsley and garlic, salt, pepper and sugar in a saucepan. Simmer over low heat for about an hour until oil floats to the surface. Add chopped basil leaves a few minutes before you remove from the flame. Allow to rest for a bit and serve with meats and pasta or dumplings.

Tomato Sauce with Pršut

1 kg tomatoes
5 dag chopped prosciutto
parsley
basil leaves
½ an onion
salt and pepper
olive oil

Fry chopped onion in olive oil with the prosciutto. Add crushed tomatoes, parsley, basil, salt and pepper. Simmer for one hour and serve on pasta or dumplings.

Parsley Sauce

3 tbsp. olive oil
2 tbsp. parsley
a little white pepper
½ lemon

Heat the chopped parsley gently in olive oil, add a little white pepper, lemon juice and pan juices from roasted meat. Bring to a rapid boil, then remove from heat. Serve with roasted meats.

Clam Sauce

1 kg clams
2 dL red wine
4 tbsp. olive oil
2 tbsp. flour
1/2 onions
1 tbsp. parsley
1/2 lemon

Wash the clams and simmer in red wine until the shells open. Remove the meat from the shells. In a separate skillet make a light roux from flour and oil. Add chopped onion and parsley, then add some fatty broth and the wine in which the clams were cooked. Simmer, then add the meat from the clams, finely chopped lemon peel and the juice from half a lemon. Bring to a boil, simmer until it begins to thicken. Season to taste with salt and pepper if necessary. This is excellent with pasta.

Sauce for Fish

6 eggs
¼ L white wine
7 dag butter
¼ L fish broth
1 lemon
2 tbsp. capers
1 pickled cucumber
2-3 anchovies

Hard boil the eggs, cool and remove the yolks (You can add the chopped whites to potato salad at another time).

Crush the yolks finely and whisk together with softened butter, white wine and fish broth. Heat over a double boiler, whisking the whole time. When it begins to thicken add the juice of a lemon, chopped pickle, anchovies and capers. Serve with poached, roasted or grilled fish.

Oyster Sauce

20 oysters
¼ L white wine
2 tbsp. olive oil
1 tbsp. flour
1 lemon
4-5 salted anchovies

Shuck the oysters and simmer them gently in their own liquor until cooked. Remove from the broth and set aside. Make a light roux from flour and oil, add a little of the cooking broth, lemon juice and finely chopped anchovies. Bring to a boil and reduce, then mix in the cooked oysters and wine. Simmer on high and reduce again slightly. Serve with fish.

Leek Sauce

25 dag leek
10 dag fat
2 sugarcubes
1 tbsp. flour or bread crumbs
broth or water
pepper

Wash the leeks very well and slice very thinly. Heat the fat and add the leeks and sugarcubes, stirring constantly. When the leeks begin to be tender, add the flour or breadcrumbs. Pour in some broth or water, simmer while stirring constantly until it begins to thicken and the leeks become very tender. Add a little pepper and serve on boiled or fried potatoes.

Lemon Sauce

10 dag butter
10 dag fine breadcrumbs
chicken or vegetable broth
1 lemon
1 egg yolk
salt

Toast the breadcrumbs in melted butter, then add a little broth and grated lemon peel. Bring to a boil, then add the strained juice of the lemon and a little salt. Simmer while stirring until it begins to thicken, then mix in the egg yolk. This is delicious with roasted fowl.

Fennel Sauce

2 tbsp. oil or fat
1 tbsp. flour
2 tbsp. fresh fennel leaf
¼ L vegetable broth
salt

Make a light roux from flour and fat or oil. When the flour begins to turn golden, whisk in finely chopped fennel and broth. Bring to a simmer, season with salt and allow to thicken a little. This is very nice on fish or fowl.

COLD SAUCES

Egg Sauce with Capers

3 eggs
parsley
1 tbsp. capers
1 salted anchovy
mustard

Hard boil the eggs and chop them very finely. Add finely chopped parsley, anchovy and capers, then stir in enough mustard. Serve with cold meats or fowl, or on sandwiches.

Cold Anchovy Sauce

8 salted anchovies
1-2 dL olive oil
1 tbsp. red wine vinegar
2-3 tbsp. water
1/2 lemon
1 clove of garlic

Clean the anchovies well, and remove the bones from the filets. Mince them very finely to a paste. Mix in a bowl with the oil, vinegar, a little lukewarm water, chopped garlic and lemon juice. This is excellent with boiled beef or mutton.

Horseradish Sauce

2 hard boiled egg yolks
2 tbsp. oil
1 tbsp. red wine vinegar
2 tbsp. grated horseradish
salt

Crush the egg yolks and mix with oil and vinegar, add grated horseradish and salt. Mix well, serve with cold beef or pork.

XI. SWEETS

Dalmatian sweets and desserts include tortes, baked and steamed puddings, cookies and simple preparations of Mediterranean fruits and nuts. A simple, dearly loved favorite is crêpes (palačinke) filled with fruit jams and compotes, chocolate, nuts, whipped cream and other delights.

A variety of small, dense cookies and biscuits (kolači) are a common addition to afternoon coffee or tea, and the tradition surrounding these on the isle of Korčula is especially renowned. There are far too many recipes to include in a comprehensive volume on Dalmatian cuisine, but a few are included here.

Tortes also tend to be dense, and recipes are often formulated around nuts and dried fruits. One favorite old recipe for a torte known as makaruli from the Dubrovnik area calls for a filling of tubular noodles.

Plum Knedli

1 kg potatoes
1 or 2 eggs
1 tbsp. shortening or butter
10 dag flour
small blue plums
breadcrumbs
butter
sugar, cinnamon

Peel and boil the potatoes, then mash them. Add eggs, shortening and flour, mix well and knead into a stiff dough, adding more flour if needed. Roll out the dough to finger width, then cut discs the size of your palm. Remove the stones from the plums and wrap each of them in dough. Allow the knedli to rest for a bit, then drop them into boiling water and cook until they rise to the surface. Drain, then roll in breadcrumbs and fry them on all sides in butter until golden brown. Sprinkle with sugar and cinnamon. Serve hot.

Coffee Pudding

20 dag butter
20 dag sugar
2 tsp. vanilla sugar
3 eggs
25 dag shortbread biscuits
brewed coffee
whipped cream

Whisk the sugar and vanilla sugar together with softened butterMix well and make 20 grams of butter, adding 3 egg yolks one by one. Beat the egg whites to a stiff foam and gently stir into the sugar mixture until all is mixed well and has an even consistency. Soak the biscuits for a short time in very strong brewed coffee and lay them in the bottom of a greased baking dish so that it is covered completely. Pour in the pudding mixture so that the biscuits are completely covered. Chill well in the refrigerator for a few hours. Garnish with whipped cream and serve.

Rice with Apples

cooked rice
½ kg apples
raisins
sugar
butter

Cook enough rice to line the bottom of a baking dish, and mix in plenty of raisins and a bit of sugar to taste. Rub the baking dish with butter and press half of the rice into it, about one finger thick. Core and slice the apples very thinly, then lay them over the rice so that it is completely covered. Sprinkle a little sugar on the apples. Lay the rest of the rice over the apples and press it down firmly. Bake in a medium oven for 45 minutes. Sprinkle with sugar and serve immediately.

Smokvenjak (Fig Cake)

1 kg dried figs
250 g almonds, lightly toasted
1 sprig of fennel
2 dL fruit brandy

Grind the figs and almonds separately. The figs should have the consistency of a rough paste, while the almonds should come to a coarse meal. Blend them in a bowl with the brandy (you may add grated lemon peel, chopped fennel or aromatic spice such as cinnamon and nutmeg for variation). Knead until the brandy is absorbed and a stiff dough is achieved. Form in the shape of round cake or smaller serving-size biscuits and dry in the oven at its lowest temperature, or bake in the sun. When cooled, press a sprig of fresh fennel into the top of the cake, wrap in parchment paper or a fig leaf and store for as long as a few months. Serve with brandy.

Fritule (Fritters)

30 g yeast
a little warm water
1½ kg of flour
1 dL brandy
3-4 tbsp. raisins
grated peel of one lemon
a handful of chopped almonds or walnuts
1 L oil for frying
vanilla sugar

Dissolve the yeast in a mug with warm water and a little sugar and flour. While leaving it to activate and rise for 15 minutes, sift flour into a bowl and mix well with hot, lightly salted water. Add the yeast mixture, raisins, lemon peel, chopped nuts and mix well, adding more warm water as needed to make a moist, yet solid lump of dough. Cover and allow to rise for one hour. Heat plenty of oil for deep frying. Drop large spoonfuls of the batter into the all and turn as needed to be sure all sides are golden brown. Drain on a plate covered with paper, sprinkle with vanilla sugar and serve hot.

Rožata (Flan)

4 eggs
12 tbsp. sugar
1 liter of milk
1 cup pear liqueur

Melt 8 tbsp. of the sugar in a little water over a very low flame, stirring constantly until you have a deep caramel color. Lightly oil the inside of a shallow bowl or pudding mold and pour the caramel into the bottom. Whisk together all of the remaining ingredients and gently pour over the cooled caramel. Cook over steam for one hour, then cool completely. Put a plate over the top of the bowl and quickly invert so that the custard releases onto the plate, and serve.

Škanjate of Brač

3 kg flour
¼ L oil
25 dag of sugar
40 g powdered yeast

Sift together the flour, sugar and yeast, then make a dough of this with the oil. You can add a little warm water to the dough, but it should be stiff. Form into a long, narrow loaf and allow to rise, then bake in a medium oven until the dough is set. Allow to cool, then slice the loaf, arrange the slices on a baking sheet and bake again at a low temperature until crunchy. Dip in wine, coffee or sherry.

Chocolate Walnuts

25 dag walnuts
25 dag caster sugar
10 dag of chocolate
1 egg white
1 cup maraschino liqueur

Finely chop walnuts, mix well with caster sugar, egg white, grated chocolate and maraschino liqueur. Form the mixture into small balls, flatten slightly and press half a walnut into the top of each. Roll in granulated sugar, allow to dry.

Cukaroni of Korčula

1 kg flour
8 eggs
25 dag sugar
25 dag butter
grated peel of one lemon
a few drops of rose extract
1 cup maraschino liqueur
10 g baking ammonia
2-3 tbsp. milk
1 cinnamon stick
powdered sugar

Separate the eggs and beat the whites to a stiff foam. Mix together egg yolks, sugar, softened butter, rose extract and liqueur, then add sifted flour and blend well. Stir in the baking ammonia with a few tablespoons of hot milk and immediately mix well, then add the foamed egg whites. Stir all together, roll out into long cylinders of about two fingers width, then cut into pieces the length of one finger. Connect the ends in a horseshoe shape and arrange on a lightly greased baking sheet with plenty of space between, as they will grow in size substantially. Bake in moderate heat until they begin to take on a nice golden color. Meanwhile, boil the cinnamon stick in water. Remove the cukaroni from the oven, brush with the cinnamon water and sprinkle with powdered sugar. Bake again until you cannot see the sugar.

Fruit Bread

14 dag powdered sugar
4 eggs
14 dag chopped dried fruits and nuts
(figs, dates, raisins, walnuts)
1 tablespoon flour + 18 dag flour
1 bar of chocolate

Foam the egg whites and set aside. Mix powdered sugar, egg yolks, chopped fruits and nuts well, then mix with 1 tbsp. flour. Blend in the foamed egg whites and mix gently. Put the mixture in a lightly greased loaf pan. Cut squares from the chocolate and arrange on top of the batter. Bake in a hot oven until it begins to brown, then cover with baking parchment, reduce heat to moderate and bake until set.

Fig Kuglice

½ kg dried figs
15 dag sugar
juice and grated peel of 1 orange
2 tbsp. rum
50 dag powdered walnuts

Grind the figs to a paste, mix with sugar, orange juice and peel, rum and walnuts. Knead well to a uniform mass, then form into balls the size of walnuts. Roll in granulated suger, place in paper confection cups and allow to dry for a while.

Figs with Honey and Wine

4½ dL dry white wine
75 dag honey
50 dag powdered sugar
1 small Mandarin orange
8 whole cloves
45 dag fresh figs
1 cinnamon stick

cream:
3 dL heavy cream
a piece of vanilla bean
3 tbsp. powdered sugar

Heat the wine, sugar and honey in a saucepan over a very low flame until the sugar has dissolved. Spike the orange with the cloves and simmer very gently with the figs and cinnamon stick in the syrup for 5-10 minutes, or until the figs are very tender. Transfer the figs and syrup to a serving dish.

Put half of the heavy cream in a bowl with a piece of vanilla bean and allow to steep for 30 minutes. Remove the vanilla, add the rest of the cream and whip together to for soft peaks. Garnish the figs with the whipped cream and serve immediately.

Figs Baked in Honey

4 large figs
3 tbsp. honey
10 dag butter
7 dag finely chopped almonds
a little rum

Cut the figs in half lengthwise. In a shallow pan heat the butter and gently fry the figs on all sides. Mix the honey with a little rum, pour it into the pan and simmer gently until the figs take up the syrup and are tender. In the last few minutes of cooking sprinkle the almonds into the pan and stir. Serve warm.

Dried Figs and Almonds

25 dag dried figs
10 dag almonds
vanilla bean
1 tbsp. vanilla sugar
1 tbsp. honey

Cut the figs into small pieces and soak them in water overnight with a sliver of vanilla bean. Grind the almonds to a coarse meal and mix them with the figs and a little of the water. Add a spoonful each of honey and vanilla sugar, mix well and serve.

Winter Kolač

15 dag dried figs
45 dag sugar
25 dag raisins
5 egg whites
20 dag of sugar
2 sheets of pastry wafer

Mince the figs and mix with raisins and 25 dekagrams of sugar. Beat the egg whites to a foam and add the remaining 20 dekagrams of sugar in the last few minutes of whipping. Gently mix the foam with the fig and raisin mixture. Lay a pastry wafer on a baking sheet and spread the mixture evenly on top, then press another pastry wafer over this to make a "sandwich". Bake at 180°C (350°F) for about 25 minutes. Cool and cut into slices.

Rice Kuglice

¾ L milk
15 dag rice
5 dag butter
8 dag sugar
small piece of vanilla bean
1 egg
breadcrumbs

Cook the rice gently in milk with the butter, sugar and vanilla until it is tender and the milk is absorbed. Spread it on a baking sheet and allow to cool. Form the rice into balls, dip them in beaten egg, then breadcrumbs, and fry in butter or oil.

Palačinke (Crêpes)

2 cups flour
2 tsp. vanilla sugar
2 eggs
3 cups milk
1 pinch of salt

Mix all of the ingredients well in a bowl to make a thin batter. Lightly oil a wide skillet and heat on a medium high flame. Pour just enough batter into the hot skillet to coat the bottom. Fry just until the batter sets and releases from the cooking, then turn and fry the other side for about a minute, or until golden brown. Repeat until all of the batter has been used, and stack the palačinke on a plate. Spread jam, fruit compote, whipped cream or any desired sweet filling or nuts onto the palačinke and roll them up before serving.

TORTES

Imotska Torta

crust:
50 dag flour
15 dag sugar
4 egg yolks
1 tbsp. butter
sherry or white wine

filling:
25 dag sugar
25 dag ground almonds
3 tbsp. rum or maraschino liqueur
grated peel of one lemon
3 eggs
1 tbsp. vanilla sugar

For the crust, sift the flour and blend with sugar, egg yolks, softened butter and sherry or white wine. Knead to a smooth dough. Roll out the crust thinly and lay it in a large, oiled pie plate. Cut the excess dough, knead and roll out again, then cut into long strips.

For the filling mix the sugar, ground almonds, liqueur, lemon peel, eggs and vanilla sugar. Pour into the crust and spread evenly. Lay the strips across the top to form a lattice. Trim the sides, bake at 150°C (300°F) for an hour and a half. Sprinkle with more vanilla sugar while still hot.

Makaruli

crust:
one egg
pinch of salt
a little sugar
50 dag flour

filling:
30 dag ground almonds
10 dag walnuts
60 dag sugar
5 dag bread crumbs
1 tsp. strong coffee
1 tbsp. vanilla sugar,
grated peel of 2 lemons,
10 eggs
25 dag butter
tubular pasta, such as penne

Mix the crust ingredients and knead to a dough and line the inside of a well greased deep cake form with it. Mix all ingredients for the filling, except for the pasta. Cook the pasta, drain and cool. Pour a shallow layer of the filling mixture into the bottom of the crust, then add a layer of noodles. Repeat until you have reached the top. Roll out the remaining crust, cover the top of the torte, seal and trim the sides. Bake for one hour at 180°C (350°C). Cool slightly, then remove from the mold. Sprinkle with powdered sugar and chopped almonds, slice and serve with coffee or brandy.

Drunken Cherry Torte

5 eggs
10 dag powdered sugar
8 dag butter
10 dag ground almonds
10 dag flour
pinch of salt
5 dag slivered almonds
1½ dL white wine
chopped lemon peel
2 cloves
2 tbsp. sugar
cherries in syrup

Mix powdered sugar with softened butter to a smooth consistency. Blend in the egg yolks one at a time, then mix in the flour, ground almonds and egg whites. Rub a torte pan with butter, sprinkle slivered almonds on the bottom, then pour in the batter. Bake in a medium oven until set. Meanwhile, boil the wine with sugar, lemon peel and cloves. Leave the cooled torte in the pan, pour over the hot wine and allow to soak. Remove from the pan, slice and serve with cherries in syrup.

Kaštelanska Torta

42 dag sugar
12 eggs, separated
42 dag almonds or walnuts
14 dag chocolate
14 dag breadcrumbs

frosting:
15 dag of sugar
3 tbsp. water
7 dag chocolate
1 dag butter

Stir the egg yolks into the sugar one by one, then blend in chopped nuts, grated chocolate and breadcrumbs. adding them one by one. Beat the egg whites to a stiff foam, then blend it into the mixture gently. Oil a cake pan and pour the mixture into it. Bake for one hour at 170°C (335°F). Remove from the pan and cool.

For the frosting, heat the sugar over a low flame with water until melted, then stir in chocolate. Remove from the heat and stir in the butter. Pour and spread this over the cake and allow it to set. Decorate with slivered almonds and grated lemon peel. You can also spread thinned jam of your choosing over the torte instead of the chocolate frosting.

Diocletian's Pogača

50 dag butter
50 dag powdered sugar
12 eggs
3 tbsp. maraschino liqueur
flour
25 dag sugar
2 eggs
chopped almonds

Blend softened butter with 50 dag powdered sugar. Add the 12 eggs and liqueur, mix and knead for approximately 30 minutes, preferably on a slab of marble in a cool place. Form into a round loaf and bake under the peka, buried in wood embers for one hour. Put the baked loaf on a plate.

Beat the eggs with 25 dag sugar, then brush the shape of an olive wreath around the loaf, and the outline of two snails facing each other in the middle. Sprinkle finely chopped almonds on the decoration, cover with the peka and bake in wood embers again until the decoration takes a nice color. Age the cake for two days before slicing. This dish is from the Roman era.

Makarska Torta

40 dag flour (fine and coarse)
3 egg yolks
20 dag butter
grated peel of 1 lemon
a little maraschino liqueur
2 tbsp. sugar

filling:
1 kg ground almonds
1 kg powdered sugar
3 tbsp. vanilla sugar
15 eggs
1 nutmeg, grated
2-3 cups maraschino liqueur
grated peel of 1 lemon and 1 orange

Sift together fine and coarse flour, blend with egg yolks, softened butter, lemon peel, a little maraschino and 2 tbsp. sugar. Knead well and roll out very thinly. Grease the bottom of a wide, shallow pie plate and line it with the pastry. Trim the excess, knead it back together and roll out thinly again. Cut into strips.

For the filling, mix the sugar and vanilla sugar, ground almonds, grated nutmeg, lemon and orange peel, eggs and liqueur. Spoon the mixture into the crust, then lay the pastry strips across the top in lattice. Trim the excess, bake for 1 hour at 170°C (335°F). Sprinkle with a little maraschino liqueur and sugar while still warm.

ABOUT THE AUTHOR

John J. Goddard is a writer, chef and cooking teacher from the United States. He currently lives in Zagreb, Croatia.

Made in the USA
Middletown, DE
23 January 2022

59455618R00163